# Courageous Pacers ™

The **COMPLETE** guide
to
# Running, Walking, & Fitness
# For Kids
(Ages 8-108)

Includes Logbook & Journal

By
Tim Erson, M.S., P.T.

Illustrated by
Michael A. Diaz

This Book Belongs To

PRO-ACTIV® Publications
P.O. Box 331186
Corpus Christi, TX 78463

Any program of exercise has inherent risk and may result in injury. Not all exercise programs are suitable for all people. It is advised that you consult your physician before starting this or any program of exercise.

The information presented in this book is not intended to replace the advice of your doctor. The author, publisher, and distributors of *Courageous Pacers: The Complete Guide to Running, Walking, & Fitness For Kids (Ages 8-108)* are not responsible for illness or injury which may result from participation in running, walking, or exercise.

*Dedicated with love:*

*To my mother, first trainer and coach,*
*Anita Erson*

*To my father, first editor and friend,*
*Fred Erson*

*and*

*In memory of*
*my good friend and teammate,*
*Michael A. Diaz*

# Acknowledgments...

This book could not have been completed without the
help of friends. It was a team effort, and many deserve thanks.

Thanks first to all my running buddies who for more than 20 years have inspired me, made me laugh, and shared their insight.

Thanks to my coaches Herb Godwin, Ray Britton, and Jay Flanagan. Thanks to you, I'm still running.

Thanks to good friends, Bob Golinski, Bob Lawrence and Marty Egal, whose positive energy has added to this book.

Thanks to Connie and Jerry Braden for your encouragement and technical support. And thanks to the Corpus Christi Road Runners Club for all you do to keep running alive and well in South Texas.

Thanks to the team at Grunwald Printing Co.

Thanks to my co-workers, Grace Gonzalez and Gracie Gonzalez, who helped prepare and organize early manuscripts, and to Denise Flores, Terry Wright, and Gloria Harper for encouragement and bearing with me.

Thanks to Danny Flores, David Marks, and Angie Allison for the photos which appear in this book.

Thanks to my readers, Buz and Karen Climis, Arlean G. Williams, Fred Erson, Barbara Edmundson, and to my student readers, Nancy Maldonado, J.T. and Kathleen Edmundson for your valuable comments.

Thanks to my friends Claude Axel, David Varga, Leszek Sibilski, and Wade Mericle for sharing your wisdom.

Thanks to friends, Eddie Roberson and Denise Flores, who helped start the first Courageous Pacers Athletic Club in 1991.

Thanks to Elsie Brunner who thought I might be a good physical therapist.

Thanks to the family of Michael A. Diaz: Nilka Trujillo, Denise and George Ortiz for your extra effort and support.

Thanks to my friend, Bea Hammons, for introducing me to Michael A. Diaz and Michelle Hammons, who designed the PRO-ACTIV® logo.

Thanks to Adam Bower who wrote the preface, and thanks to the many children I've had the privilege to serve. *Your courage, comments, and ideas are what fill the pages of this book.*

Thanks to my family for many years of love and encouragement. Thanks, Mark, for your support, and thanks, Sue and Scott, for your "tips" and presentation ideas.

And thanks, a million thanks, to the person I love who cheered me on and devoted countless hours to typing, laying out, and editing this work. Thank you my beloved wife, talented co-worker, training partner, and best friend, Paula.

# Contents

**Preface**

# What
# The Courageous Pacers Athletic Club
# is All About

### by Adam Bower

The Courageous Pacers Athletic Club is about kids walking and having fun.  It gives them a lot of exercise, and it helps them build up their muscles.  I think the Courageous Pacers Athletic Club is good for kids to get their body to work out.  It's fun because you get to race, walk, and meet new people.

We walked at Heritage Park in the road and people cheered for us.  I feel happy going across the finish line.  The end is fun, having the drawing for prizes.  These races help me to walk farther and get a lot of exercise.  I can't wait until the next race.

—August, 1993

Adam is a 4th grade student at Galvan Elementary School in Corpus Christi, Texas.  He competes regularly in community road races and fun runs with the Courageous Pacers Athletic Club in Corpus Christi.

## Please Read

Any program of exercise has inherent risk and may result in injury. Not all exercise programs are suitable for all people. It is advised that you consult your physician before starting this or any program of exercise.

The information presented in this book is not intended to replace the advice of your doctor. The author, publisher, and distributors of *Courageous Pacers: The Complete Guide to Running, Walking, & Fitness For Kids (Ages 8-108)* are not responsible for illness or injury which may result from participation in running, walking, or exercise.

## Introduction

# Getting Started

It takes courage to be a kid these days. It takes courage to learn new skills—to say, "I think I can"—to move your life positively and confidently in a direction of fun, challenge, adventure, and change.

Today a growing number of kids show courage by entering community running, racing, and walking events. Through practice and participation, these kids are becoming winners.

In Corpus Christi, Texas, the Courageous Pacers Athletic Club was founded in 1991. A program of running, walking, and fitness, it has helped children achieve personal and athletic goals.

This book invites you to join the fun.

## To begin

1) Get excited about the benefits of exercise and being in good physical condition.

2) Read chapters 1-5, and learn how to get started.

3) Find a partner, and begin a month of easy walking or running, 3-5 times a week, 15-20 minutes a day.

4) Set goals. Use your logbook and journal.

5) Look for upcoming races, fun runs, or walkathons in your area. Plan to enter one.

6) Train, read, write. Encourage others, and have fun.

An international circle of friends welcomes you.

See you at the races,

*Tim*

**Chapter 1**

# Running Tips

S-T-R-E-T-C-H

## COME ON, LET'S PLAY!

No matter what you choose, these words really mean, **Come on, let's have *fun!***

Running and walking are ways to have fun—ways to play—ways to move when you're excited.

Whether you're new to sports or consider yourself an old pro, running and walking are activities that will help you grow strong and become your best, physically and mentally.

## Exercise . . . Running, Walking . . . Fun!

Running and walking are more than just exercise. Through them, you strengthen your heart and lungs, burn excess fat, improve your posture, increase your metabolism, and think creatively.

Children learning to walk, run, or jump do so with smiles on their faces because they know that exercising, *playing actively,* is fun. Running and walking improve fitness and provide a basis for sports training and active living.

This chapter will introduce you to the world's oldest and most popular sports. You'll find them challenging and exciting as well as safe, convenient, and all natural. Enjoyed by people of all ages, they offer skills at which you can improve easily.

What's your favorite thing to do?

What do you do when you play?

What do you consider *active* play?

Have you ever made up a game on your own, or with friends?

Did you make up your own rules?

There aren't too many rules you have to follow to be a good runner or walker. Getting the most from your training, racing, and play is as easy as following "Seven Super Tips" in one simple word.

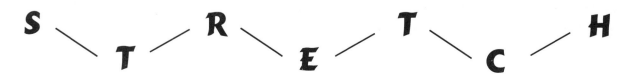

## Prepare to S - T - R - E - T - C - H

> *Anything worth doing is worth doing right.*

This is an old saying my father used. It holds true for games you play, projects you do, and ways you choose to exercise or have fun.

Doing something right means taking the time to get yourself ready. Preparing, physically and mentally, is what successful athletes do no matter what their sport. Stretching, warming up, eating right, and keeping an eye out for safety is part of an athlete's routine to perform well and prevent injury.

Many athletes use special equipment in their sports. If you're a runner or walker, your *body,* your arms and legs, your heart and lungs are the special equipment you use. Shoes and clothing are important, but they're not what you depend on for success.

## You're the best thing you've got going for yourself.

—Claude Axel

What do *you* think of that? What does it say to you about fitness and exercise?

Exercise is not something someone else can do for you. What you do and don't do for yourself really *does* matter.

# S - T - R - E - T - C - H

*Seven super tips in one simple word.*

**S**TRETCH  **S** = START and finish your workouts with exercises to warm up and cool down.

Warm Up!  Cool Down!

s**T**RETCH  **T** = TEAM up with a friend. Don't run alone. Make sure someone always knows where you are.

st**R**ETCH  **R** = REST if you have pain. It's your body's way of saying you may need to *slow down* or take the day off.

str**E**TCH  **E** = EAT *after* you run, not before. Food in your belly can cause cramps or stomach upset during exercise.

## STRE**T**CH   **T** = TAKE precautions when the temperature is hot or cold.

| *Hot Days . . .* | *Cold Days . . .* |
|---|---|

Drink water before and after you run.

Wear layers of clothing. A knit hat and gloves helps you stay warm.

Run during the cool part of the day.

Do a good warm-up.

Wear a light-colored hat or visor.

Avoid getting wet.

Stop running if you feel dizzy or light-headed.

## STRET**C**H   **C** = CLEAN UP after you COOL DOWN.  Take a bath or shower, and put on clean, dry clothes.

## STRETC**H**   **H** = HOW did you do? Enter it in your logbook and journal.

Timothy E. Erson ©1993

15

# Chapter 2

***E****verybody and everything that moves needs to stretch.*  It's the first thing you do when you get up in the morning, and it's what you continue to do throughout the day.

**Ding-a-ling-a-ling!**
Reach out your arm,
turn off the alarm.

Now, think for a second,
what planet you're on.

Push up to the ceiling,
then wiggle your trunk.
Straighten your legs.
Now—out of the bunk.

Push yourself up, and sit at the side. With a groan and a yawn, let your mouth open wide.

Now you're stretched, now you're ready, now up out of bed.

**Ready,**

  **and Set,**

    **Start** the day just ahead.

## Why Stretch?

Did you ever wonder why dogs and cats, turtles and clams stretch at the start of a day? All living creatures stretch. Look carefully, and you'll even see flowers and trees stretch open petals and leaves at the first glimpse of morning sun or after a heavy rain.

Why?

Because stretching unlocks a muscle's energy. It loosens stiffness and readies it for activity. Stretching warms and warns a muscle before work or play. Stretching is important when you've rested all day.

## Warm-ups and Cool-downs

*Warming up* is the way athletes begin workouts. Muscles do better when they ease into exercise. Allowing oxygen and nutrients to flow to muscles helps increase their energy. Warming muscles before exercise keeps them flexible and can prevent injury.

Exercise *after* a workout is called a *cool-down*. Cool-downs keep blood flowing through muscles—they keep them from feeling stiff. Do each warm-up and cool-down exercise *s l o w l y*. Hold a stretched position comfortably for several seconds. That's the key to doing it correctly.

## Which Muscles Should Be Stretched?

Running and walking involve your whole body. Your head, neck, arms, trunk and legs all need to be stretched before exercise. Don't forget to warm your heart—it's a muscle too.

When you stretch, *start at the top and work your way down.* On the pages which follow, you'll find exercises for your head, arms, trunk, legs, and feet—and one for your heart.

If you have questions or need help doing exercises correctly, talk to your coach or P.E. instructor. They can give you good advice and may be able to show you additional exercises for the Coach's Corner on p. 23.

## Stretching Tips
to get You
**Ready,** and **Set,** to

1) **Start at the top and work your way down.**
   Stretch your body from head to toe.

2) **Hold a position comfortably for several seconds.**
   Think of how you stretch when you get up in the morning.

3) **Don't overstretch.** Overstretching hurts and can cause muscle injury. Stretching exercises shouldn't hurt.

4) **Don't b o u n c e your way through an exercise.**
   Bouncing like a yo-yo may tighten or injure a muscle. Move slowly through each exercise.

# STRETCHING EXERCISES

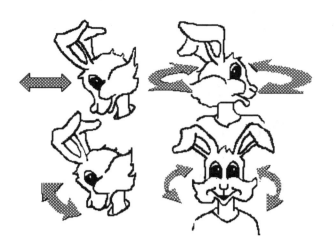

**(1)**

## HEAD ROLLS
Move your head slowly to the right, left, side to side, up and down.

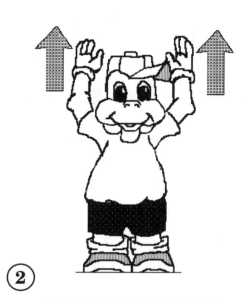

**(2)**

## REACH FOR THE SKY
Breathe in as you push your arms high. Exhale as you lower them. Repeat 6-8 times.

**(3)**

## ARM CIRCLES
Forward, then back.
30-40 seconds in each direction.

**(4)**

## SIDE BENDS
Do each side 2-3 times.
Hold for 15-20 seconds.

⑤
## TRUNK ROTATIONS
Turn body to each side slowly.
Repeat 4-5 times.

⑥
## LUNGE STEP
Bend front knee forward, keeping
back leg straight. Dip low 2-3 times
on each side, holding the position.

⑦
## QUAD STRETCH
Hold ankle with one hand, and
steady yourself with the other.
Repeat each leg 2-3 times.

⑧
## RING SITTING
Sit with feet together.
Press knees down. Hold.
Repeat 3-4 times.

**⑨ HAMSTRING STRETCH**

Sit or stand. Keep your knees straight, and reach for your toes. Hold 20-30 seconds. Repeat—legs together and apart.

**⑩ CALF STRETCH**

Keep back leg straight and foot flat. Feel a stretch in the back of your lower leg. Repeat 2-3 times each leg.

**⑪ ANKLE CIRCLES**

Turn your foot around and around. Repeat 8-10 times each leg.

**⑫ MARCH IN PLACE or do JUMPING JACKS**

Do 10-20 repetitions to get your heart muscle ready.

# COACH'S CORNER

Use this page for additional exercises.

## E - A - S - Y

**E**verything that moves needs to stretch.

**A**lways start and finish your workout with stretching exercises.

**S**tart at the top, and work your way down.

**Y**o-yo's are no-no's. Stretching exercises are best done slowly without bouncing, without pain.

Timothy E. Erson ©1993

23

# Chapter 3

# Dress Wisely

## S - T - R - E - T - C - H

## With Comfort

# The Emperor's New Clothes

*by Hans Christian Anderson*
*retold by Timothy E. Erson*

Long ago, there lived a great emperor, or king. One day, a crafty tailor brought new clothes to show the king. He claimed that the clothes could only be seen by those who were very clever or wise. He said that they were woven from a special material. In truth, he hadn't brought any clothes at all—only empty boxes.

The king, certain of his own great wisdom, requested that the clothes be brought to him. The tailor and his assistant opened their boxes and pretended to show the clothes. "How beautiful the garments are," they remarked. "How splendid they'd look if Your Majesty tried them on." The king saw nothing. But, not wanting to appear unwise, he agreed to try them on. He even mumbled that they were magnificent.

The story goes on to tell how the king's subjects reacted when they saw him parade before them in only his underwear. Most bowed silently. Some smiled, but only the smallest dared to laugh out loud because none wanted to appear foolish or unwise.

## Using Your Head to Dress Your Body

Dressing *wisely,* not dressing to be wise, is what most people do every day. Wearing colors and patterns you like helps you look and feel your best. *You use your head* to make choices about clothes for school, play, and special occasions.

Athletes choose clothes that help them look good, feel comfortable, and stay protected. Being clever about what they wear in different weather or training conditions keeps athletes from getting sick or injured.

## Knowing What To Wear

There are two important questions to ask yourself when choosing clothes for a run or walk.

1) Are the clothes comfortable?

2) Are they correct for the weather?

Colors and styles change. But choosing wisely for comfort and weather means ***wearing the right stuff on the right day.***

## Comfort

Comfortable clothes are lightweight and give you freedom of movement. Choose fabrics you like that are soft and breathe easy. Close fitting tights or sweats that aren't baggy cut wind resistance and let you move freely in the cold. Avoid clothes that rub or blister skin.

# CLOTHES TO HUNT FOR WHEN IT'S . . .

### Cold

Wear layers of clothing. An extra t-shirt, long-sleeved t-shirt, or light jacket makes it easy to *peel off* layers as your body heats up. Use a knit hat, mittens, or socks on your hands to keep body heat in.

### Warm

Run during the cool part of the day. Avoid hot and humid conditions which are dangerous. Wear light-colored clothing, sunscreen, and a light hat or visor to help you stay cool. Drink plenty of water before, during, and after your run.

### Rainy

Water resistant outer wear helps in light rain or drizzle. Consider shortening a rainy day workout so that you don't get cold or end up sick. A warm shower, dry clothes, and hot drink soon after a run will warm you.

### Twilight

When you run at twilight, the hours close to sunrise or sunset, wear light-colored clothing and/or reflective wear. Drivers have trouble seeing you when the sun is low, so be careful. Learn to W-A-T-C-H O-U-T. (See pages 38-39).

# TEMPERATURE & TRAINING WEAR

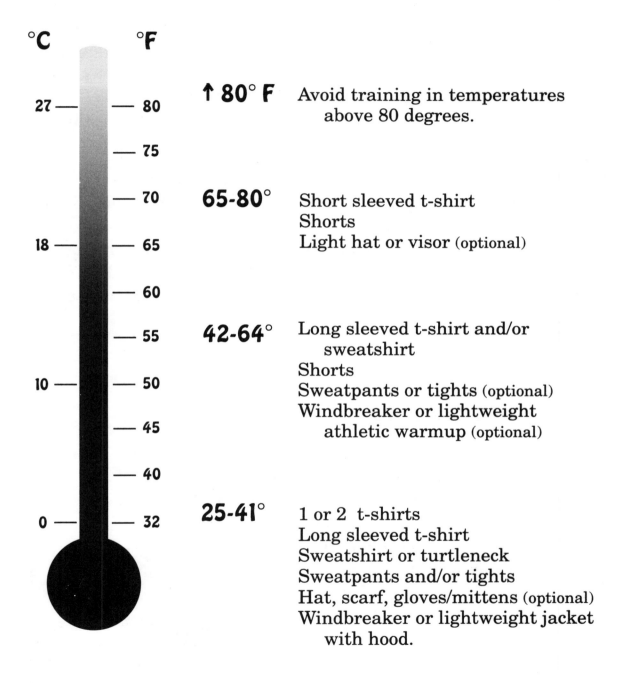

°C    °F

27 — — 80     **↑ 80° F**   Avoid training in temperatures
      — 75                   above 80 degrees.
      — 70     **65-80°**    Short sleeved t-shirt
18 — — 65                    Shorts
                             Light hat or visor (optional)
      — 60
      — 55     **42-64°**    Long sleeved t-shirt and/or
10 — — 50                       sweatshirt
                             Shorts
      — 45                   Sweatpants or tights (optional)
                             Windbreaker or lightweight
      — 40                      athletic warmup (optional)
0 — — 32       **25-41°**    1 or 2  t-shirts
                             Long sleeved t-shirt
                             Sweatshirt or turtleneck
                             Sweatpants and/or tights
                             Hat, scarf, gloves/mittens (optional)
                             Windbreaker or lightweight jacket
                                with hood.

**P.S.**  Dress cool.  Running and walking produce body heat.  Consider
clothes you'd wear if the temperature was 10 degrees warmer.  You'll
be more comfortable and sweat less if you dress a little cool.

## Shoes and Socks

Shoes should be comfortable, lightweight, flexible, and provide good cushioning. Look for *road shoes* if you train on hard surfaces. Shoes with a rigid, or sturdy, *heel counter* give support when landing. *Track* shoes are lighter weight and generally used for speed work or racing. They may not offer the support you need for training on roads. *Lace locks* or *elastic laces* are used by many runners to keep shoes from coming untied.

Wear clean socks every time you go out for a run. Choose socks that are light-colored and made with acrylic or acrylic blends. Some dark socks have dyes which may get into your skin. Socks can be cushiony or flat, long or short. You decide which ones look and feel best. Socks made of 100% cotton get wet when your feet sweat and may cause blisters.

## The Recognizable Bag

Find a bag that's easy to recognize, and take it to races or when training away from home. Use it to carry your sweats, clean t-shirts, a towel, band-aids, sunscreen, extra socks, a summer or winter hat, and a plastic bag for laundry. (It's also a good idea to pack extra toilet paper in case the portable toilets are out).

## Keep Your Clothes Clean

When the workout's done
> and you've had some fun,

When your clothes are sweaty
> and they start to feel heavy

Think for a moment—*What can I do?*

Find a washing machine—*That'll make 'em like new.*

Dressing wisely means putting clean clothes on a clean body. You'll look better, feel better, and stay healthier if you take time to stay clean.

**Chapter 4**

# Where to Run

S-T-R-E-T-C-H
&
W-A-T-C-H  O-U-T !

*VAR SKA VI GÅ?*
*(Where shall we go?)*

That's what my relatives in Sweden say when they get together for a walk or run. After that, they have a *long* discussion and make a decision on which route to follow. For people in Sweden, and for millions around the world, running or walking around the neighborhood, in parks, or on trails in the woods is a favorite pastime.

One of the best features of running and walking is the freedom you have to choose from a variety of places to train. Courses that are challenging, safe, and new can be found almost anywhere. Your *playing field,* your *court for fun,* can be just about wherever or whatever you want it to be.

Designing a course isn't hard, but it does take some practice. Good courses encourage you to run or walk them again and again. Indoors or out, around a building, or around the block, at school or in the park, in your neighborhood or at the mall—only your imagination will limit the number of places you'll find to train. It's easy to *get in shape* and *stay in shape* when you've found the right course for you.

## Common Courses

Two of the most common types of courses are pictured below.

### Out and back

Run from a starting point out, and then back over the same route.

### Loop

Run around an area such as a park, field, or several blocks of your neighborhood.

## Timing Your Course

Timing yourself with a stopwatch helps you determine if a course is too long or too short. Using a watch again and again on a course also lets you know if your speed has improved.

Beginners can use a watch and try to run or walk for 10 minutes without stopping. Choose a direction, follow it for 5 minutes, then turn around, and head back over the same route. Keep a steady pace, and you'll arrive back at your starting point in 10 minutes.

When you're in better shape, try a 20 minute workout. Head out for 10 minutes, turn around, and finish over the same course. Trained athletes can do 30, 40, or 60 minute courses using the same method.

## Favorite Courses

Everyone finds a favorite time and place to train. I like to run early mornings in summer and prefer sunny afternoons in winter. The places I enjoy most are trails in parks and open scenic areas. Surrounded by natural beauty, I'm happy to be outdoors and active.

## Counting Laps on Short Loops and Tracks

Near my parents' house, a 78-year-old man walks 16 laps a day on the high school's 1/4 mile dirt track. He is a kind man and smiles hello to all who pass by.

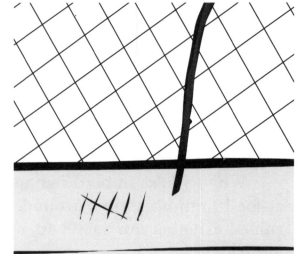

When he arrives, he leans his walking stick against the fence near the track's outer lane. Each time he completes a lap, he takes the stick and draws a line in the dirt. When he's drawn 16 lines, he smiles widely and heads home, satisfied that another four mile workout is complete.

On the same track, a lady carries a *lap counter*. On it, she pushes a button each time she completes a lap. Since the device adds laps for her, she is free to let her mind wander and think creatively while she walks.

Some people use the *pebble drop* method to count laps. They start by picking up pebbles equal to the number of laps they plan to run. Each time they complete a lap, they drop a pebble, until there are no pebbles left.

A *pedometer* can also be used to tell you how far you've gone. It's a device that I call an "odometer for people." A pedometer clips onto your waist. Instead of counting laps, it counts your *steps* and adds their distance. I got my dad one for his birthday—he tells me it works great when he walks in the neighborhood.

*Counting aloud* is perhaps the easiest and most common way to count laps on a short course. Saying a number each time you begin a lap lets you hear and remember how many laps you've completed.

## Measuring Courses

Find out the distance of your courses to help you plan workouts and figure mileage.  Some courses are premeasured so you'll know the number of laps per mile.  High school tracks are 440 yards, or 400 meters, which is equal to 1/4 mile.  To complete one mile on a 1/4 mile track, go around it 4 times.

In schoolyards, on playgrounds, or in local parks, measured courses are often known by P.E. instructors, city park workers, or local Road Runners Club members.  Contact one of these people to find out if a course has been set up near you.

If you don't have a track, measured park or playground, then make up a course, and measure it with the *odometer* on a car, bicycle, or calibrated wheel.  Short courses less than 1/4 mile can be measured by two people with a 100-foot measuring tape.

## Figuring Laps on a Short Course

The conversion table below shows the number of laps per mile for many short loop and indoor courses.

| COURSE DISTANCE | | # OF LAPS |
|---|---|---|
| YARDS or | FEET | PER MILE |
| 440 | 1320 | 4 |
| 293 | 880 | 6 |
| 220* | 660 | 8 |
| 176* | 528 | 10 |
| 160* | 480 | 11 |
| 147 | 440 | 12 |
| 73 | 220 | 24 |
| 18 | 53 | 100 |

*typical indoor track sizes

FORMULA TO FIGURE LAPS PER MILE:  | 5,280 FEET | ÷ | # OF FEET IN ONE LAP | = | # OF LAPS PER MILE |

# W A T C H

***W**atch for cars.* *Face traffic so that you can see cars coming.* Drivers won't always see you, especially near driveways, intersections, curves, or when the sun is low.

***A**void busy roads.* Less crowded roads are safer, and the air you breathe is cleaner.

***T**rain in daylight.* Wear light-colored and/or reflective clothing close to sunrise or sunset.

***C**yclists share our roads.* Be cautious and considerate. Cyclists travel on the same side of the road as cars.

***H**eadphones are dangerous*—avoid using them. Keep your *eyes and ears open* when training near traffic.

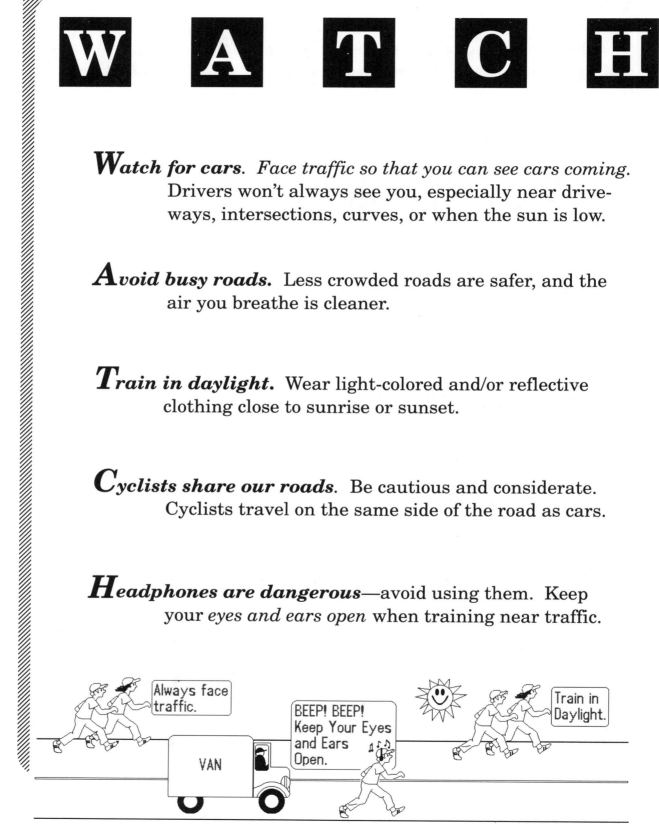

Always face traffic.

BEEP! BEEP! Keep Your Eyes and Ears Open.

VAN

Train in Daylight.

**O**bserve traffic signs and signals. Stop at traffic lights. Jog in place to maintain momentum and stay warm.

**U**nderstand, but stay clear of dogs. They bark most if you come near their property. Move slowly and steadily away from them.

**T**rack!—When practicing, move to the right if a faster runner behind you calls out, *Track!*

Timothy E. Erson © 1993

39

**Chapter 5**

# Taking Off with the ~~Right~~ Wright Stuff

## S - T - R - E - T - C - H
## Your Dreams

**Wilbur Wright**

**Orville Wright**

**MACHINES CAN'T FLY!** That's what many people believed when the Wright brothers thought of building the first airplane.

No one offered them money to try, and they had no background in engineering, but the two bicycle mechanics from Dayton, Ohio believed they could do it. After four years of planning, practice, and patience through many failed and a few successful experiments, they finally came up with an invention they called the *Wright Flyer I*.

Handmade from canvas and wood, with propellers mounted behind the wings, it looked a little different from today's planes. But the basic design and ideas which made it fly are the ones still used in airplanes today.

The *Wright Flyer I* was first tested at Kitty Hawk, North Carolina, on December 17, 1903. On that cold, windy day, the brothers flew it four times. The first flight lasted 12 seconds and went 120 feet. Their final flight was 59 seconds and traveled 852 feet.

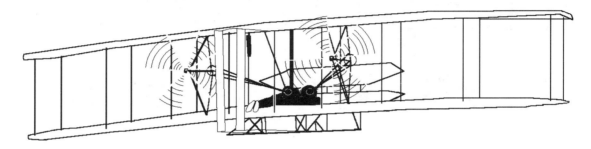

Having accomplished their goal, they dreamed bigger, and the next year built the *Wright Flyer II*. A stronger, larger craft, it flew for 5 minutes. As their knowledge and expertise increased, so did their dreams. In 1905, the *Wright Flyer III* flew magnificently around a farm field for a record 39 minutes.

Thousands were inspired by what the brothers had done—their dream of flight had become real. In 1927, Charles Lindbergh flew *The Spirit of St. Louis* non-stop from New York to Paris in 33-1/2 hours. In 1932, Amelia Earhart flew in record time from New Foundland, Canada, to Ireland, becoming the first woman to solo the Atlantic.

## Airplanes and Athletes

Athletes, like early aviators, set goals and work toward them. Sometimes, obstacles must be overcome, but those who keep trying find ways to succeed. When you first try to run long distances, it might seem hard—your body's motor may want to slow down or quit after just a few strides. If you need to, take a rest. The important thing is that you begin and make a plan to build on what you've got.

Set small goals at first. As you gain knowledge and experience, you'll pass those goals and learn how to accomplish bigger ones. Perhaps you'll find, like early pilots, that you can go distances and perform feats that you may never have dreamed possible.

Sixty-five years after the Wright brothers flew at Kitty Hawk, astronauts landed on the moon. It didn't happen all at once—it was a series of many small goals and brave attempts that made that dream a reality.

I'm glad the Wright brothers had the courage to believe in themselves—to not give up on their dream. Today, all of us benefit from their discovery. Can you imagine what the world would be like if people hadn't learned to fly? If Wilbur and Orville hadn't had the courage to try?

## Taking it to the Top

The Wright brothers experienced many ups and downs on their journey to flight. Finding a way to get 700 lbs of man and machine safely through the air began by observing birds, flying kites, and building gliders.

In preparing to realize your dreams as an athlete and in life, be prepared for ups and downs, for setbacks and leaps. All are part of the journey to making a dream come true.

## G + 3P = S

Do you have a dream?  What do you hope to accomplish?
Become enthusiastic about your dream, and turn it into a goal.  Use
the formula, G + 3P = S, and add to it imagination, hard work, and
fun.  Use this formula to make your dream come true.

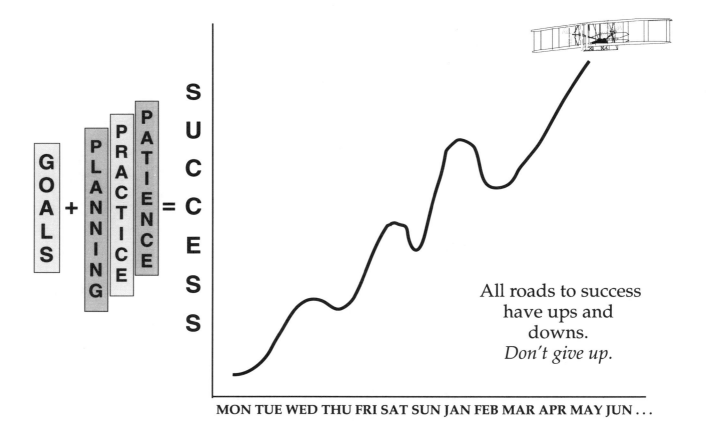

| Goals | + | Planning | (takes imagination) | = | S U C C E S S |
| | | Practice | (means hard work) | | |
| | | Patience | (learn to keep it fun) | | |

# How high can YOU fly?

GOALS + PLANNING PRACTICE PATIENCE = SUCCESS

All roads to success
have ups and
downs.
*Don't give up.*

MON TUE WED THU FRI SAT SUN JAN FEB MAR APR MAY JUN . . .

Timothy E. Erson ©1993

## Turning Your Dreams Into Goals

There is nothing more important to success than a dream. Take time to think about your worthwhile dream. Write it down, and make it your goal. Develop a plan, and work on that plan a little each day. Some dreams take a long time. Let your dream guide you, and work to make it come true.

My dream, my goal, is: _____

_____

_____

## Making a Plan—Training Goals and Racing Goals

On pages 46-47, learn how to write training, racing, and fitness goals. Use the charts to pick an item from each of the four columns, and make a sentence that will become your goal. Do it in pencil so that you can revise and change the goal easily. Let each sentence begin with the words, **I will ....**

Make daily goals simple, and be flexible. Choose a goal to work on each week, and write it on the **Training Goal** line of your log page. See the example in the Sample Log on page 154.

## TRAINING GOALS (Your Plan of Action)

| Activity | How Much? | How Often? | How Long? |
|---|---|---|---|
| I will run<br>I will walk<br>I will do<br>I will _____<br>other exercise | _____<br>distance<br><br>_____<br>minutes<br><br>____ strengthening<br>exercises<br>____ stretching<br>exercises<br><br>_____<br>speed work/intervals | on MWF<br>(Mon Wed Fri)<br>on TThS<br>(Tue Thr Sat/Sun)<br>every day<br><br>____ times per week<br><br>_____<br>other | for 1 week<br>for 1 month<br>for 3 months<br>for 6 months<br><br>_____<br>other |

Examples: **I will** run / 20 minutes / 5 times per week / for 1 month.

**I will** do / 5 strengthening exercises / on TThS / for 3 months.

**I will** walk / 2 miles / on MWF / for 2 months.

I will _____

_____

I will _____

_____

I will _____

_____

46

## RACING GOALS

| Activity | How Far? | How Well? | When? |
|---|---|---|---|
| I will run<br><br>I will walk<br><br>I will _____<br>(swim or bike) | _____ meters/yards<br>_____ K (kilometers)<br>_____ mile(s)<br><br>_____<br>other distance<br>or course | in _____<br>time<br><br>at _____<br>place | in 1 week<br>in 1 month<br>in 3 months<br>in 6 months<br>in 1 year<br>in __ years<br>_____<br>date |

Examples:  **I will** run / 5K / in less than 25 minutes / in 6 months.

**I will** walk / 1 mile / in 15 minutes / in 1 month.

**I will** run / around the park / at the youth race / in 3 months.

I will _____

_____

I will _____

_____

I will _____

_____

47

Chapter **6**

# Strengthening Exercises

S - T - R - E - T - C - H

Your Power

L - I - F - T

**O**ne thing humans do well is find ways to make jobs easier.

When a man or woman first invented the wheel, little did they know that it would lead to invention after invention after invention. In an effort to make life easier, our inventiveness has led to an age of electronic and laser technology. Today, work is often as easy as pushing a button.

What's your favorite invention? Mine is the washing machine. Can you imagine how long it would take and how hard it would be to wash all your clothes by hand?

Your body has been wonderfully made to become stronger through physical activity. Through activity, muscles become conditioned and coordinated for a variety of skills. They perform tasks faster and with greater ease. The question children and adults face today is: If work keeps getting easier, how will their muscles develop the strength they need?

## Do Runners and Walkers Need Strengthening?

Running and walking adds strength and endurance to your legs and heart muscle. But what about your arms and trunk? These areas need strength to power you when racing, climbing hills or enduring long distances.

Can you think of other reasons to have strong arm and trunk muscles? What about for other sports? What about to keep good posture? What about for helping others and taking care of yourself?

## Making Muscles the Old Way

Our ancestors developed a lot of strength just by doing the everyday chores needed to survive. Homes were heated by wood that was carried or coal that was shoveled. Water for bathing and washing clothes had to be carried from a well or stream. A trip to the store or day at school meant walking and carrying groceries or books.

My grandmother came to America from Finland in the 1920's. She was the superintendent of a four-story apartment building in Brooklyn for more than 20 years.

To heat the building and provide hot water, my grand-mother had to shovel coal. She also cleaned and made difficult repairs. In the spring, she carried earth and supplies to her flat rooftop and enjoyed planting a garden of fresh vegetables and flowers.

My grandmother was proud of her strength and skills and often told us, **Hard work is good for you, and lots of it.**

## What Do Your Muscles Think of Hard Work?

Muscles *love* hard work. They *ache* to be exercised. They want to be strengthened and used. Muscles need attention from you as much as you need strength from them. If a muscle's power isn't used at least 2 or 3 times a week, it loses power and gradually becomes weak.

Through activity, muscles are nourished—cells are strengthened and able to store more energy. Strong muscles *metabolize* food better and keep you from storing excess fat.

*YOUR MUSCLES*
*ache*
*TO BE EXERCISED!*

Energy and self-confidence get a boost when you use your muscles daily. Exercised muscles look better, feel better, and learn to work better too.

---

and there's more . . . **Tendons and Ligaments**

Exercise does more than make strong muscles. Tendons, which attach muscle to bone, and ligaments, which attach bone to bone, are also strengthened and able to handle heavier loads. Runners and walkers can avoid many injuries by having strong tendons and ligaments.

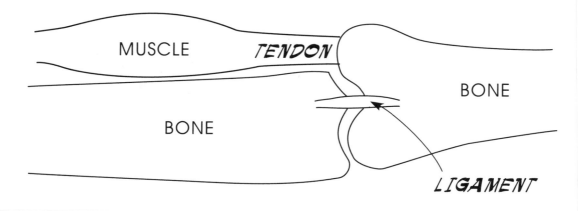

MUSCLE    *TENDON*

BONE

BONE

*LIGAMENT*

## Adding Leg Power

To add power and strength to your legs, pick one day a week to run up hills. Running into a strong wind also works to develop leg strength and power.

Cycling, jumping rope, kicking a ball, swimming with a kick-board, and climbing stairs instead of taking an elevator are ways to strengthen your legs outside of running and walking.

## Strengthening Exercises

Many athletes like to do arm and trunk strengthening at the end of a run or walk. Cooling down from a run can be a good way to warm up before lifting. It's a good idea to lift with a partner in case one of you gets hurt. (See the L-I-F-T chart on pages 54-55).

## Weights

Start with light weights, and increase gradually. Find weights that are easy to grasp and safe to use. Dumbells and cuff weights are good choices.

If you want to make a weight, find a plastic detergent bottle with an easy-grasp handle or a 16-20 oz. plastic soft drink bottle. Filled with water or sand, they make good weights to strengthen your arms.

| Plastic Bottle | Filled With Water | Filled With Sand |
|---|---|---|
| 16 oz. | 1 lb. | 2 lbs. |
| 24 oz. | 1 1/2 lbs. | 3 lbs. |
| 32 oz. | 2 lbs. | 4 lbs. |
| 48 oz. | 3 lbs. | 6 lbs. |

# L - I - F - T

### Light weights first

Use light weights when you start a strength program. Pick a weight that you are able to lift through the exercise 10 times.

### Increase gradually

Increase the number of repetitions and sets first. Increase the amount of weight later. Build strength gradually to reduce your risk of injury.

### Five exercises

Learn to do exercises which strengthen different muscle groups. Keep breathing when you exercise. Blow air out when you lift a weight, and take air in as you lower it.

### Three times a week

Exercise your upper body at least three times a week. Do the five exercises shown above or choose some other good strengthening activity. Here are some ideas:

# Your Strengthening Exercise Guide

Light ——————> Heavy

(2.2 lbs = 1 kilogram)

Use plastic bottles only.

16 or 20 oz.          Easy-grasp

| 1st month | | | | | | |
|---|---|---|---|---|---|---|
| S | M | T | W | Th | F | S |
| | | | | | | |
| | | 5 exercises | | | | |
| | | 10 repetitions | | | | |
| | | 1 set | | | | |
| | | | | | | |

| 2nd month | | | | | | |
|---|---|---|---|---|---|---|
| S | M | T | W | Th | F | S |
| | | | | | | |
| | | 5 exercises | | | | |
| | | 10-12 repetitions | | | | |
| | | 2 sets | | | | |
| | | | | | | |

| 3rd month | | | | | | |
|---|---|---|---|---|---|---|
| S | M | T | W | Th | F | S |
| | | | | | | |
| | | 5 exercises | | | | |
| | | 10-15 repetitions | | | | |
| | | 3 sets | | | | |
| | | | | | | |

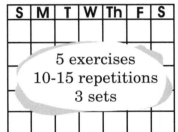

PUSH-UPS          OVERHEAD PRESS          BICEP CURLS          SIDE-LIFT (PALMS UP)          CRUNCH-UPS (ARMS IN FRONT)

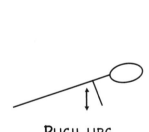

FLY A KITE IN STRONG WIND

GYMNASTICS

SHOOT BASKETS          yard work

ROW A BOAT

CLIMB ON MONKEY BARS

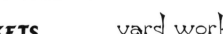
wash a car          Park Fitness Trail

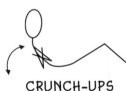

Swim

Timothy E. Erson © 1993

55

# Chapter 7

# Logbooks & Journals

## S-T-R-E-T-C-H

## Your Journey

**D**o you know anyone who uses a logbook? Logbooks are important sources of information to people on the go. Pilots, truck drivers, ship captains, car owners, and athletes use logbooks.

## What is a Logbook?

A logbook, or *log*, is a record of a journey. Early explorers used ship logs to record information about their travels overseas. Included were facts about the weather, stars used for navigation, uncharted lands, and dangerous reefs.

Many captains and crew members kept *journals*, as well. They described details of discoveries made, people they met, and stories about life at sea. From these ship logs and journals, saved long after a ship and its crew were gone, we have learned much about exploration and history.

## Logbooks and Journals:  What's the Difference?

Logbooks record facts. Journals, like diaries, include thoughts, adventures, funny stories, and interesting ideas.

Runners use logbooks to record times, places, and distances run. Sometimes they add facts about the weather, body weight, and heart rate. Since athletics is a journey and adventure, athletes often combine log and journal information.

## Athletes, Logs and Journals

Runners and walkers are known for keeping logbooks and journals. Many have saved records of their athletic training and experience for years.

Swimmers, cyclists, and triathletes also keep logbooks, and baseball players are meticulous recorders of hitting and fielding percentages. For each, logbooks and journals are training tools which tell a personal story.

## *Thoughts for Your Journal*

Ideas come to people who run or walk. Henry David Thoreau, a famous American writer and walker, wrote, "When my feet move, so do my thoughts."

*Creative thoughts* will be an interesting and surprising part of your running and walking experience. There is a connection between body, mind, and movement which generates new ideas and energies.

Whenever you travel, take along your logbook and journal. Training in new places brings new thoughts and adventures. Exploring their environment is something runners and walkers do well.

## Using the Log Pages

Use pages 156-255 as your logbook and journal. Each log page is set up for one week's worth of training data, and opposite is a journal page which includes a thought for the week. Pages 257-263 offer a Race Log to record the events in which you participate.

# Logbooks Answer Questions About Training

### *How often should I train?*

Train 3, 4, or 5 days a week, and give yourself 1 or 2 days to rest. Make training a regular part of your week's activity.

### *When is the best time to train?*

Early morning or late afternoon is best for most people. Remember to schedule enough time for warm-ups and cool-downs.

### *When should I write in my logbook?*

The best time is soon after you've cooled down and cleaned up. Some people do it in the evening. What's important is that you find a regular time and place, just as you do for training. Think of workouts and races as not complete until they've been recorded.

### *Suppose I miss a few days or weeks of training?*

Once in a while, we all miss several days or weeks of training because of an injury, bad weather, scheduling conflicts, or because our bodies need a rest. A training log will tell how much you've missed.

If you've stopped exercising for a long time, begin again easy. Rebuild endurance and speed gradually. This will help you to regain strength with less risk of injury. The most important thing is that you *do* start again. *Don't let your off season be longer than your on season.*

## TTT (Tim's Training Tip)

The longer you stick with running, walking and writing, the greater your benefits will be. Make training a habit, and continue to make fitness part of your life year round. Be a body that can:

### *Think fit, Be fit and Stay fit*

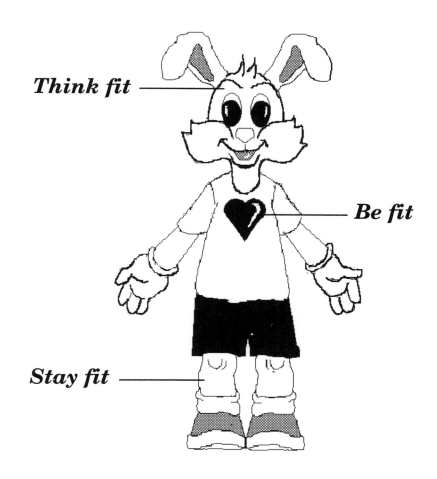

Think fit

Be fit

Stay fit

**Chapter 8**

# Training Partners

S - T - R - E - T - C - H

## Your Enjoyment

**T**radition says that when he saw an apple fall from a tree, Isaac Newton was inspired to investigate the laws of gravity and motion. His observations are the basis of what we know about how and why objects move.

Newton was a scientific genius and found that, throughout the universe, *Bodies in motion tend to stay in motion while bodies at rest tend to stay at rest.* He also discovered that to get resting bodies moving, something was needed to give them a push. Somehow, energy had to be added.

Newton's laws of motion are universal. What he described for heavenly bodies is true for our own bodies as well. To get them moving, there must be a push. For us, that push is called *motivation*.

## What Motivates You?

. . . What gets your body in motion?

Two things have motivated me year after year.

1) The great feeling I get after a run,

   and

2) the people I've met who make training and racing fun.

Knowing how great I'll feel after exercise doesn't always work to get me started, but training with family and friends usually does. Planning to meet others for a workout motivates me and keeps me from putting it off until tomorrow.

## What are Your Reasons to Train?

 Put a check by 3 motivators on page 65 that are important to you.

# Running/Walking ...

____ is good for my health.

____ introduces me to new friends.

____ helps me train for races.

____ gives me new ideas.

____ gets me in shape for other sports.

____ burns excess fat.

____ gives me confidence.

____ helps me relax.

____ is fun!

____ is something I enjoy with friends.

____ lets me enjoy a time of peace and quiet.

____ makes me feel good.

____ helps me look good.

____ adds excitement.

____ gives me something to improve at.

____ is something I like to do with my family.

____ is something I am good at.

____ lets me explore new places.

____ helps me sleep better.

____ gives me a coach or adult friend to look up to.

____  _____ .
　　　(other)

## Training Alone or In Groups

Training alone or in groups makes running or walking both an individual *and* team sport. With others, you often go farther, faster and more consistently than you would on your own. Training partners add to your fun and safety.

Training by yourself lets you enjoy the peace and quiet of a long, solitary run or walk. Some days, athletes choose to be alone when they workout. But on other days, a training partner is absolutely necessary to help get you out when you'd rather be in. If you train alone, do it in a safe place, and make sure someone always knows where you are.

## Where Do You Find Partners?

You'll be surprised how easy it is to find training partners. *Running and walking are contagious.* Just start exercising, and let a few people know you're out there. Before long, people will ask if they can join you.

Most people know that exercise is good for them and look forward to having a partner. Like you, they want to have a body in motion. Friendships formed through running and walking grow deep and can last a lifetime.

## Pets as Partners

Norman Kelly, a racer from Zavala Elementary School in Corpus Christi, suggests taking a dog, either your own or your neighbor's, when you go for a run or walk.  Dogs love to run and need exercise as much as we do.  Be sure to take a leash, and plan ahead for your pet's safety as well as your own.

## My Training Week

Each week, I train for about 6 hours including warm-ups, workouts, and cool-downs.  That leaves me 162 hours to do everything else.  The distance I go varies, but the amount of time I give it is usually the same.

| Day | Distance (Time) | Strengthening |
|---|---|---|
| M | 30 minute run or lap swim with my wife. | L-I-F-T |
| T | Interval training on track with friends. (see Ch. 12) | |
| W | 30-40 minute easy run. | L-I-F-T |
| Th | 60 minute fartlek run. (see Ch. 12) | |
| F | Rest. | |
| S | 45 minute run or race. | Yardwork, wash car, other sports |
| Su | 60-75 minute long run with friends. | |

## Let's Compare:

# TRAINING ALONE  &  WITH OTHERS

| | | |
|---|---|---|
| Gives you quiet time to think and be creative | — | Workouts include good conversation and fun |
| Lets you choose the most convenient time | — | Information is shared about running, racing, & training |
| Lets you choose your own pace | — | You often run faster and farther with partners |
| Lets you choose your own training place | — | Motivation, consistency, and safety improve |

***Both have advantages.***
***Both are part of an active running and walking life.***

## One More Reason to Have Training Partners:

*Friends get you out when you'd rather be in*
*They get you up and help you begin*
*They say, "Let's go!" when you feel, "Oh, no!"*
*Training with friends; it's the best way to go.*

(Sing this poem to the tune of your favorite song.)

TTT

Ralph Waldo Emerson, a walker and writer, wrote, **The only way to have a friend is to be one.**

Be a friend to someone by inviting them to join you for a run or workout. If the person goes the same speed and distance as you, then work together at common goals. If your partner goes slower and prefers shorter distances, invite him or her to join you on your easy day or as part of a long warm up or cool down. Partners can also join you on a bicycle or roller skates.

A good way to improve your speed and endurance is to find a partner who runs somewhat faster than you. Athletes can motivate one another by working together on difficult goals.

# Chapter 9

# Wilma Rudolph

## Courageous Olympian

*Meet Wilma Rudolph, a talented and courageous athlete, whose heroics on and off the track have inspired millions.*

*But first, let's talk about the Olympics.*

# The Olympics

Every four years, the world celebrates the Olympic Games. In a different city each time, the tradition of ancient Greece brings together the world's greatest athletes for competition in a spirit of friendship and peace.

The first Olympics was held in Athens, in 776 B.C. The Games included running, and later, horse racing, wrestling, boxing, and the pentathlon (five track and field events) were added. The Olympics represented the best in sports competition and celebration.

The ancient Games continued every four years for more than 1000 years. They were festive and brought together friends and many former enemies. The Olympics celebrated people's ability to compete and play peacefully. In 393 A.D., the Games ended when Emperor Theodosius abolished what had been a long and worthy tradition.

A movement to revive the Games after 1500 years was led by Baron Pierre de Coubertin of France. A nobleman and educator, he hoped the spirit of the Games would promote better understanding between nations. In 1896, thirteen countries accepted the invitation to compete at the first modern Games in Athens.

Today the Olympics is the world's greatest sports event. It attracts thousands of athletes from around the world and includes summer and winter games. Baron de Coubertin is remembered with gratitude as the Father of the Modern Olympics.

## Wilma Rudolph and the Modern Games

In 1960, the Olympics were held in Rome. Wilma Rudolph, a 20 year old sprinter from Tennessee State University was a member of the U.S. Team. It was her second Olympiad. In 1956, she had been the youngest member of the U.S. Team that traveled to Melbourne, Australia.

In Rome, Wilma won three gold medals. She was considered the Games' outstanding female athlete. But, for Wilma, winning races, even running or walking short distances, had not always been easy or even possible to do.

## Growing Up

● Clarksville
● Nashville

Wilma Rudolph was born on June 23, 1940. She came from a large family and grew up in Clarksville, Tennessee. Wilma was often sick as a child and at age 4 became seriously ill with scarlet fever, double pneumonia, and polio. Her family feared that she would not survive.

Blanche and Ed Rudolph, Wilma's parents, brought her to a hospital in Nashville, 50 miles away. One of her legs was severely weakened by the polio, and doctors wondered if she'd ever walk again. Her parents were taught to massage and exercise the leg and were given a metal brace to help support it. With the help of her brothers and sisters, a routine of massage and exercise was followed four times a day.

Growing up with active brothers and sisters was hard for Wilma. She could not always keep up and often felt left behind. While the others ran and played outside, Wilma often stayed alone inside and cried. Eventually, she decided she'd had enough. She wanted to play and was determined to test her leg. She would try to be successful, *no matter what.*

She started by bouncing a ball and shooting baskets in the yard. Eventually, she was brave enough to join the other kids for games. Even though she was not the fastest player or highest scorer, Wilma's mother encouraged her effort, saying, "Do your best, and you win."

## New Shoes

At age 11, Wilma's leg was becoming stronger. She found that in the house she could walk short distances without having to wear a brace. Her parents helped celebrate her improved strength by giving her new shoes one Sunday as the family was getting ready for church. Wilma's parents were happy that day, and Wilma was especially happy. Wearing new shoes meant she no longer had to wear the hospital shoes that held the heavy metal brace.

In her teenage years, Wilma continued to grow tall and strong. She worked at being athletic and was determined to do her best. She joined the girl's basketball team and eventually became its highest scorer. Wilma also ran track and was a top sprinter.

## Her Talents Develop

One day, Tennessee State University Track Coach Ed Temple saw Wilma play basketball. He was impressed with her skill and invited her to be part of his summer running program for girls. There, Wilma met other women track athletes who were busy training for national and international competition.

At Coach Temple's camp, Wilma's running improved. She was invited to Seattle and qualified as a sprinter for the U.S. Olympic Team. Her contribution as a member of the Women's 4 x 100 m Relay* at the Melbourne Games earned her a bronze medal. She returned to Clarksville a hero.

After returning from Australia, Wilma graduated from high school and enrolled at Tennessee State University. There, she continued to run as a Tennessee State "Tigerbelle" under the guidance of Coach Temple.

## The Rome Olympics

In 1960, Wilma qualified for her second Olympic team. Coach Temple was named Head of the U.S. Women's Track and Field Team. Wilma and her teammates were pleased because that meant he would be with them in Rome. They trained diligently and prepared for the challenge ahead.

In Rome, the day before her first qualifying run, Wilma was practicing and accidentally stepped into a hole on the field. She sprained her ankle. Coach Temple and the U.S. Team worried that she might not be able to compete.

Wilma, however, did compete and made it to the finals in all her events. In the Women's 100 m final—a race to determine the world's fastest athlete—Wilma won by 6 meters. In the 200 m final, Wilma again placed first and won a second gold medal. In her final event, the Women's 4 x 100 m Relay, Wilma ran the anchor leg. Her determined effort helped bring a world record victory to the U.S. Team and gave her a third gold medal.

* 4 x 100 m Relay is a 400 m race in which each of four athletes carries a baton 100 meters, passing off to the next athlete. Each leg is 100 meters. The final leg is called the *anchor leg*.

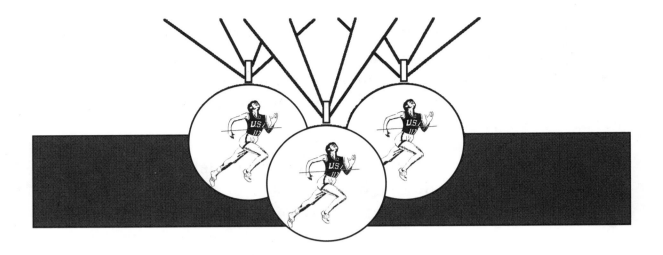

## Ambassador to the World

After an exciting Olympics in Rome, Wilma and her teammates traveled through Europe with Coach Temple to competitions in London, Athens, Amsterdam, Cologne, and Berlin. She was an international star, sought after by reporters and fans alike. The world loved her, and she was hearalded *Queen of the Track.*

## Athlete of the Year

In 1961, Wilma received another outstanding honor. She was invited to Washington, D.C., where President Kennedy gave her the Sullivan Award as the nation's top amateur athlete.

As an adult, Wilma married her high school sweetheart and raised four children. She has been a spokesperson for civil rights and created *The Wilma Rudolph Foundation* to help children in need lead active and fulfilling lives.

An outstanding athlete, an ambassador of goodwill and sportsmanship, Wilma Rudolph will forever inspire people determined to do their best and succeed against great odds.

## Author's Note

A courageous heroine at the 1992 Olympics in Barcelona reminded me of Wilma Rudolph. Gail Devers, a 100 m finalist, had also been a member of the U.S. team in 1988. In 1990, she was diagnosed with Graves Disease and nearly lost her legs to amputation. Devers, however, fought hard to come back and qualified for the 1992 U.S. Team. Her effort showed tremendous courage and spirit. In a race that was the closest Women's 100 m final in Olympic history, Devers won the gold medal.

To learn more about Wilma Rudolph and other courageous athletes, talk to your librarian.

# Chapter 10

# Aerobics & Form

## Relax . . . and Stride . . .

It's amazing when you think about the number of people who enter and complete marathons. In cities around the world, thousands of people train for these 26.2 mile events every year. In New York, host to one of the most popular U.S. marathons, there is a waiting list for athletes who want to enter.

| Marathon | Entrants |
|---|---|
| Boston | 9,000 |
| Grandma's (MN) | 6,000 |
| Honolulu | 30,000 |
| Houston | 5,000 |
| Los Angeles | 19,000 |
| Mexico City | 20,000 |
| New York | 27,000 |
| Toronto | 4,000 |
| Washington, D.C. | 13,000 |

Today, we associate the word "marathon" with endurance. But in 490 B.C., Marathon was the name of a village in Greece. Near it, a battle was fought, and the Greek army, greatly outnumbered, was victorious. To spread the news of victory, legend says that a soldier named Pheidippides (fī dip´i dēz´) was ordered to run from Marathon to Athens. Although he was tired from battle, Pheidippides ran the 24 mile distance as ordered. When he reached Athens, he shouted his message, "Rejoice, we conquer," then collapsed and died.

As a race, the marathon was part of the first modern Olympics at Athens in 1896. Spiridon Loues, a Greek shepherd trained for the event while chasing sheep over the countryside. He finished first on a course similar to the one run by Pheidippides and became a national hero.

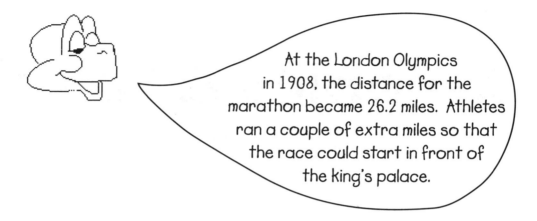

At the London Olympics in 1908, the distance for the marathon became 26.2 miles. Athletes ran a couple of extra miles so that the race could start in front of the king's palace.

## Why is Marathoning So Popular?

More than a race, the marathon is an event that celebrates people's ability to push their bodies and minds to new limits. It takes many months and even years of training to complete such a distance. But, for all who participate or watch, the marathon is truly inspiring.

You may wonder, "How can people run such long distances?" The answer has a lot to do with what athletes know about *aerobics* and *form*. Practicing these techniques when you train can help improve *your* distances too.

# Part I: Aerobics — the Great Refresher
## What does "Aerobics" mean?

When you hear the word, *aerobics,* what do you picture? Do you imagine groups in colorful clothes exercising to the beat of their favorite songs? Aerobic dancing is a lot of fun, and many people do it to stay in shape. But there's more to the word, "aerobic." *Aerobic* means *with oxygen,* and to athletes, *exercising with oxygen.*

Running, walking, biking, hiking, swimming, and jumping rope are all exercises that can be done aerobically. The most important thing is to do the activity long enough and hard enough for the heart and muscles to get a strong, steady workout. Pacing is moderate and breathing, controlled. Aerobic exercise should be done for at least 20-30 minutes, five times a week.

## Finding Your Aerobic Pace

*ON YOUR MARK—GET SET—GO!* Take off at top speed. How far do you think you'll go? Most people, even world class sprinters, don't get too far. Muscle fibers used in top speed running work well for short bursts but not for long distances. When their explosion of energy is over, you feel out of breath. This is because your heart and lungs must keep pumping oxygen so that your muscles can recover and recharge.

*ON YOUR MARK—GET SET—SLOW!*

*This is aerobic—don't take off too fast.*
*The secret here—see how long you can last.*
*Your heart rate goes up as you begin to breathe deeper.*
*But at this moderate pace, you're not getting weaker.*

*To know if it's right, just ask yourself this:*
*"Can I talk while I run, or are there words that I miss?"*

Aerobic exercise reduces body fat and strengthens the *cardiovascular system.* It moves you toward a healthy size and weight with less risk of injury. No matter what shape you're in or what your experience has been, YOU can improve with aerobics.

## Living the Aerobic Life

Being aerobically fit helps you, not only in sports, but in all areas of life. Because it's good for your body, aerobic training is also good for your mind. The good feeling that comes after an aerobic workout is uplifting and energizing. Though your body feels sweaty and hot on the outside, aerobics makes you feel clean and cool on the inside. Aerobic activity can make your thoughts more cheerful and ordered.

*Aerobic exercise...*

*refreshment to your body and your mind.*

# Part II: Good Form — Cruising with Control

## Relax . . . and Stride . . . Relax . . . and Stride . . .

Good form is easy when you feel good. But when you get tired, your body may become tense, your legs feel heavy, and your form begin to sag. When good form goes, so goes that good feeling.

To pick yourself up and get back into smooth stride, *start by forcing a smile.* No matter how bad you feel or how slow you go, a smile can ease pain and start to give you a lift.

Next, let your mind start talking to your body. Tell it to *relax . . . and stride . . . relax . . . and stride . . . .* Say the words over and over. Sing it to the tune of your favorite song. Soon, your head will rise, and your back will straighten; your arms will relax, and your stride will strengthen. As you begin to look good, you'll start to feel better, and when you start to feel better, you'll start to move better too.

This technique, called *cruise control* was introduced to me by my friend David Varga, a Corpus Christi marathoner and track coach. It really works.

# Relax . . .

## UPPER BODY . . .

**Keep it centered.**

### Head
Keep it straight. Not too high; not too low.
Let your jaw drop and your mouth be open
slightly.

### Shoulders, arms, & hands
Arms should swing comfortably from the
shoulders *and* the elbows.
Avoid bending your elbows too much.
Shape your hands as if holding a cup or pencil.

### Trunk
Move your body forward, not up and down.
Keep it centered over your pelvis.
Let air flow in and out of your lungs easily.

# . . . and Stride . . .

## LOWER BODY . . .

**Keep it smooth.**

*Stride* means to move your legs smoothly
and comfortably while supporting a
relaxed upper body.

### Hips & Knees
Let your movements be natural and light.
Use your body's momentum to help lift and
carry you along.

### Ankles & Feet
For long distances, land on your heels, and
push off your toes.
Adjust and shorten your steps for uneven
or slippery ground.

## Your Form vs the Earth's Form

Sometimes when you train, it's not 60 °F with low humidity, no wind, on a flat surface. Training in a variety of conditions is what most people experience. It's one way you're able to have new adventures and develop different strengths.

### Hills

Uphill, pump your arms and lean into it. As you climb, shorten and quicken your steps to increase power. When you reach the top, relax your arms, take a few long strides, and work out the stiffness.

Running downhill should be done cautiously. Drop your arms to give them a rest. Control your speed to reduce shock and injury.

### Slippery and Uneven Ground

Mud, ice, and other slippery surfaces signal *slow down* and *watch your step*. Avoid traffic or winding roads after a light rain or drizzle. Shorten your steps for a safer, smoother stride.

### Wind

Wind at your back is not usually a problem. Most runners like wind at their backs (except when it's hot and humid).

Moving *into* the wind is tough but offers many training benefits. On warm days, it cools you, and always it works to improve strength and power. Approach a headwind as you would an uphill. Lean forward, pump your arms, and shorten your steps to increase power.

On cold days, be aware of the wind chill factor. Do loop courses, or out and backs with the wind at your side. Avoid open and unprotected areas.

## Heat and High Humidity

Heat and high humidity are dangerous to athletes. In hot weather, train indoors or during the cool part of the day. Drink water before, during, and after a hot run. Plan a lighter, easier workout.

> If you need help fine tuning your form, ask a knowledgable coach or P.E. instructor to watch you run.

TTT

Many runners are familiar with the term, *Second Wind*— a feeling of renewed energy in the middle or at the end of a workout. Interestingly, it can happen on days when you may not feel like exercising but choose to do it anyway.

Even a lazy day can end up a great day. Aerobic pacing while you . . . relax . . . and stride . . . can help you feel lighter, faster, and more in control. Renewed, you'll experience the *Second Wind.*

# Chapter 11

# Choosing a Race

S - T - R - E - T - C - H

## Your Opportunity

**H**ave you seen ads for races, walkathons, or fun runs? These events, popular throughout the year, take place in cities, large and small. Even the smallest towns have annual races associated with festivals and holidays.

Distances and fees vary, but community races, walkathons, and fun runs are for everyone. You won't have to look far to find events that are challenging and just right for you.

SAVE OUR PARK

*Clean-up Walk*

Name
Address

**Holiday Race**

**5K Run/2 mile Walk/ Youth Mile/Kids 1/4**

*This run is one of the most fun of the year. Run at the beach with the wind howling and seagulls flying, there will be plenty of food for your senses . . .*

*Age Group Relays*

*includes: Youth-Masters Teams*

Team Captain
Members

## How to Find Races

Information about races is available through local Road Runners Clubs, City Parks and Recreation Departments, newspaper ads, and at stores that specialize in runners' shoes and equipment. If you run for a club or at school, a schedule is likely to be provided.

Here are some popular events where I live. Similar events can be found almost anywhere.

**Corpus Christi Calendar of Events:**

Mar    Goodwill's "Day Break" Run/Walk

Apr    March of Dimes Walkathon

       YMCA Twilight Run

       CROP - Walk Against Hunger

May    South Texas Sports Medicine Run/Walk

       **Beach to Bay** 26.2 Mile Marathon
              Relay

July   *Fleet Feet's* ® "Four for the Fourth"

Sept   Bayfest Runs—5K & 15K

Oct    Rehab Fest 5K Run/2 mile Walk & Roll

Nov    Alzheimer's Association Walkathon

       Thanksgiving Day Turkey Trot

Dec    Toys for Tots 5K Run/2 mile Walk

One of the best ways to stay motivated is to pick an upcoming race and prepare for it. Make plans to be in a race even if it's still several weeks or months away. Thinking about a race keeps you focused and consistent when you train.

**How *far* should I race?** | How far you race depends mostly on what you've been doing in practice. Avoid choosing distances that are more than twice what you've done recently. Long or short, any race offers excitement and challenge if you give it your best effort.

**How *often* should I race?** | Enter as often as you like. If possible, give yourself a week between long and hard race days.

## Racing Partners

A racing partner can be anyone you run near in a race. It may be a friend or family member. It may be someone who just happens to be running at the same speed as you. Partners help push one another to do their best.

Watch for groups that race together and form "packs". It's exciting to see or be part of a group of athletes that carry one another through strong and steady pacing.

## Beating the *Butterflies*

An upcoming race is exciting, but you might also feel nervous as the time and day of an event draw near. Rarely do athletes go to the line without some knots or "butterflies" in their stomachs. New racers may think they're the only ones who feel them, but they soon learn that when the starter's gun goes off, so do the butterflies.

## Injured or Unable to Race?

If you are injured or just not feeling well enough to race, don't worry—you can still be part of the action. If you know in advance that you'll be unable to run, check your application, and call the information number to find out how you can help as a volunteer. Races depend on the support of many volunteers.

If you are not needed as a volunteer, attend anyway. Cheer for those who are running. Let them know how much you enjoy their effort. There are lots of great ways to stay involved with your sport.

**TT**T

Experienced racers have a distance which they like to do best. You'll find a favorite race distance too. Run an event again and again to learn how to run it best, but be open to the challenge of trying new events.

Running distances you're not familiar with may offer some surprises. Longer distances improve endurance, and shorter runs improve speed. Enter other race distances occasionally, and see what a difference it makes when you go back to your favorite event.

**Chapter 12**

# A First Race
# &
# Better Ways to Train

S - T - R - E - T - C - H
Your Experience

**W**hen I was 14, I entered my first race.  A freshman in high school, I'd been a member of the track team for two weeks.  In my mind, I was a sleek, up-and-coming Olympic hopeful ready to burst onto the scene.

The coach entered me in the quarter mile (440 yards), and I was confident I could do well.  I imagined placing high and winning an award.

A cold, clear Saturday in December marked my debut.  Our team traveled from Hightstown, New Jersey, to an indoor track in Jersey City.  Athletes from around the state gathered, and a parade of colors warmed up around the 220-yard track painted on a hard wood floor.

My race was not scheduled until the afternoon. I had never been to such an event, and I felt nervous. I was careful not to eat too much and made sure I drank just enough water. In my nervousness, I stretched and jogged continuously so that my muscles would be loose and I'd be ready when it came time to run.

At 3 o'clock, my name was called. I lined up with five other 14-year-old boys. At the sound of the gun, we took off sprinting, and I fell in line behind three early leaders. I was amazed at how fast they could go. Though I ran as fast as I could, I was just barely able to stay with them.

At the end of the first lap, the leaders began to pull away. Moving into the second lap, my breathing became deep and labored. Suddenly, one of the two runners behind passed me on the back straightaway. I tried to stay with him but was losing speed. Still, there was one runner behind, and I was determined to hold my place and finish the best that I could.

Into the final curve, my legs started to feel heavy. I had only 60 yards to go but was moving slower and slower. In runner's terms, there was a "bear on my back" or, as my teammates would say, "rigor mortis" was setting in.

Friends cheered as I struggled to hold on. Spots, which now circled in front of my eyes, grew larger as the runner behind moved closer. In a final effort, I lifted my head and leaned forward. Then, in what seemed an eternal instant, my eyes closed, my knees buckled, and my body fell. I fainted.

I crashed, but momentum carried me, and I slid on the hard wood floor. The runner behind continued. In perfect stride, he stepped up and leaped, sailing over my body and across the line. On the floor, arms outstreched, I laid flat—just a few feet short of the finish.

Friends who stood cheering moments before came onto the track. They picked me up and carried me across the line. Because I needed their help, I was disqualified.

I sat with my coach and soon recovered. He asked if I was alright. He told me that perhaps I went out too fast and maybe I needed to work on my endurance. Then, he said,

TIM, I THINK NEXT RACE, WE'LL TRY YOU IN THE MILE.

I smiled, and as I turned to join my teammates, I thought . . .

A MILE . . .? I CAN'T EVEN MAKE A QUARTER.

*Not too long after that, my coach showed me . . .* (turn page)

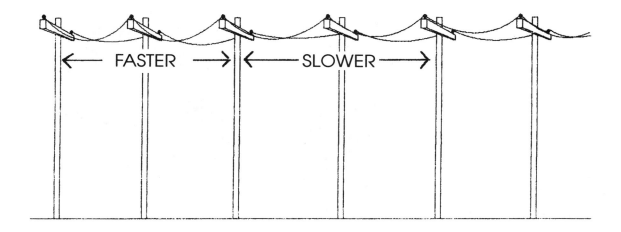

FASTER            SLOWER

## Better Ways to Train—Intervals & Fartlek

You can use intervals and fartlek to build endurance and speed. Many runners do one or two such sessions a week to maintain and improve racing skills.

### Intervals (formal)

*Intervals* refer to sets of fast and slow runs over a certain distance. Athletes can do short or long intervals depending on whether they train for speed or endurance. The most popular interval distances are 200, 400, and 800 meters.

Typically, interval work is done on the track. A workout listed as 4 x 400 m indicates four sets of fast runs, each followed by a recovery jog of the same length. Since interval training involves fast running, do a good warm-up, and complete at least one month of distance training before you attempt it.

If you don't have a nearby track, use a stopwatch, phone poles, or other markers to help you do intervals. Using a watch, run hard for 60-90 seconds, then jog easy for 3-4 minutes. Repeat. Using phone poles or other markers, do sets of fast runs past 2, 3, 4, or 5 markers, then jog easy over the same distance.

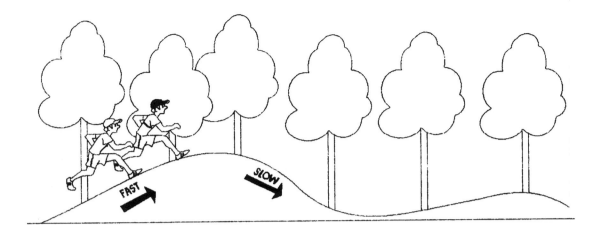

## Fartlek (informal)

*Fartlek* is a Swedish word that makes Americans laugh. To Swedes, it means *speed play*. Runners everywhere have found it a good technique to improve power and speed while having fun on a run. Beginners use fartlek to combine running and walking and to improve their endurance. Seasoned athletes use it to build speed by running some parts of a course fast and others easy.

Speed play can be done anywhere, with distances and courses that vary. On hills, go up fast and come down slowly. In parks, run fast across fields and go easy on trails. On long, flat roads, use phone poles or road markers to make up fast and slow sequences. Run to one marker slowly, then steadily increase your speed as you pass each of the next four or five. Repeat speed play sequences again and again.

*With imagination and planning, it's easy to use intervals and fartlek to achieve goals of running longer, faster, and with greater ease.*

Chapter **13**

# Miles & Meters

## Today's Quiz

1. Which distance is considered a mile?
   a. 1,000 paces marched by a Roman soldier
   b. 5,280 feet
   c. 8 laps on the ancient Olympic track in Athens
   d. all of the above

2. Which distance is raced by men and women at the Olympics?
   a. the U.S. mile
   b. the 1500 meter
   c. 10 furlongs
   d. all of the above

## One Mile—How far is it?

Depending on who you talk to, a *mile* could mean something different in terms of distance. In the United States, a mile is equal to 5,280 feet.

### The First Mile

The word, *mile*, comes from the Latin word, *mil*, which means *one thousand*. Roman soldiers marching long distances counted 1,000 marched paces as a mil (or mile). A pace was counted when the right foot hit the ground, swung through the air, and then landed on the ground again. An average pace was 5 feet, and so 1,000 paces (a mil) was equal to 5,000 feet. Soldiers knew that if the distance from Rome to Pompeii was 150 mil, they would have to march 150,000 paces to get there.

> 1 mil = 1,000 paces
> 1 pace = 5 feet
> 1,000 paces = 5,000 feet

### The First Olympic Mile

In ancient Greece, one lap around the Olympic track in Athens (209 yards) was called a *stadia*. Eight stadia was about equal to one Roman mil. Eight laps on that track eventually became known as a mile.

In the English language, the Greek word *stadia* became *stadium*, and the Roman word *mil* became *mile*.

### The Modern Mile

In England during the 1500's, people continued using the Roman mile to measure long distances. Many farmers, however, measured plowed fields in row lengths called *furlongs*. One furlong was equal to 660 feet. Since 660 did not divide easily into 5,000, Queen Elizabeth I changed the distance of a mile to 5,280 feet. One mile, then, equaled eight furlongs.

# Meters

The metric system was developed by French scientist Gabriel Mouton in 1670. Today, at international sports competitions and in science, the metric system is more commonly used than the American and British system of feet, yards, and miles.

In many countries, athletes use meters and kilometers to log their training. A meter is about three inches longer than a yard, and 1000 meters is called a kilometer. At the Olympics, all races are run in meters. The 1500 m, referred to as the *metric mile,* is 119.57 yards shorter than a U.S. mile.

Today, more and more races are being named for their metric value. In training, however, most U.S. athletes still use miles to log their weekly distances and for race splits. (A split is your time at a specific point in a race. Usually, splits are called out at mile intervals on long distance runs in the U.S.)

**On the chart below, compare meters, yards and miles. An asterisk (*) indicates that the distance is raced at the Olympics.**

| meters | (yards) | miles (approximate) |
|---|---|---|
| 100 m* | (109.36) | 1/16 M |
| 200 m* | (218.72) | 1/8 M |
| 400 m* | (437.44) | 1/4 M |
| 800 m* | (874.88) | 1/2 M |
| 1,000 m  (1K) | (1093.60) | .62 M |
| 1,500 m* | (1640.40) | .94 M |
| 1,600 m | (1749.76) | 1.0  M |
| 3,000 m* | —— | 1.88 M |
| 3,200 m | —— | 2.0  M |
| 5,000 m* (5K) | —— | 3.1  M |
| 8,000 m  (8K) | —— | 5.0  M |
| 10,000 m* (10K) | —— | 6.2  M |
| 42,195 m* (42.2K) | —— | 26.2  M (marathon) |

## The Mile as a Race

The mile is not run at the Olympics, but it remains a favorite for spectators and competitors. It's a race that combines speed and endurance and pushes athletes to challenge per-minute-mile barriers. Many of track's great legends have been milers. A few are noted below.

## Roger Bannister

On May 6, 1954, Roger Bannister ran the most famous of all miles. A medical student and former British Olympian, Bannister set his sites on becoming the first person to run a mile in less than four minutes. His time of 3:59.6 broke a nine-year-old world record and achieved what was once thought impossible.

## Glenn Cunningham

Called the "Iron Man of Track", Cunningham at one time held world records in the mile and 1500 meter. An athlete from Kansas, he set national age group records in high school and ran in two Olympiads during the 1930's. Cunningham took up running to strengthen his legs which were severely burned and nearly amputated as a result of a schoolhouse fire at age seven.

## Jim Ryun

Jim Ryun, in 1964, became the first high school student to run a mile in under four minutes. At 17, he qualified for his first of three U.S. Olympic Teams. At 19, he set a world record in the mile, running it in 3:51.1 on a dirt track. His time stood for nine years as the fastest mile ever run.

## Kipchoge Keino

A policeman from Kenya, "Kip" Keino was one of the first in a long line of record holders from Kenya. Keino competed in three Olympiads and won gold and silver medals in the 1500 m at Mexico City and Munich. A versatile athlete, he also won a silver medal in the 5000 m at Mexico City and a gold medal in the steeplechase at Munich.

## John Walker

One of the longest career milers, John Walker of New Zealand ran a mile in 3:49.08, to become the first person to break 3:50. At the Montreal Games, he won the gold medal in the 1500 m. Walker was the first to run more than 100 sub-4 minute miles over an 18 year period.

### T T T

The mile is a great training and racing distance. Improving at it takes a combination of speed and endurance. Many distance runners figure their training and racing pace by how many minutes they run per mile.

For beginners, the mile is often a first training goal and mark of success. Have you logged your first mile? If so, congratulations. If not, plan a *strategy* to do it. Be part of an athletic tradition that has produced legends.

Answers to *Today's Quiz:*

2. b

1. d

**Chapter 14**

# The Pre-Race Meal

S - T - R - E - T - C - H

Your Energy

M O-O-O-VE BACK!
IF I EAT A HAMBURGER, I'LL
RUN LIKE A HAMBURGER.
I NEED **PASTA** TO HELP
ME RUN **FASTA**.

Hamburger Hare

**T**ake it from me—I must have been nuts the day I ate nuts just hours before running a race. I found out the hard way that eating half a bag of peanuts is probably the worst thing a person can do before starting a long, hard run. The first mile went O.K., but after that, my belly rebelled. I felt cramps for the rest of the race and then the whole night through. I've learned that there are better choices than peanuts when planning a pre-race meal.

## ATHLETES AND FOOD

Athletes and coaches have always been interested in how food affects performance. Most know not to eat too much before a practice or contest, but what *can* athletes eat to help them do their best?

Long distance runners know that foods packed with *complex carbohydrates* provide the most efficient and long lasting fuel for muscles. Complex carbohydrates are a better source of energy than protein or fat because they require less oxygen for each calorie burned. For runners who have carbohydrates stored in their muscles, more energy is available for every breath taken.

*Spaghetti and rice, potatoes and bread* are rich in complex carbohydrates and are by far the most popular foods eaten by athletes the night before a race. Pasta parties are today's pre-race tradition for marathoners.

## GOOD FOOD AND YOU

Physically and mentally, what you put into your head and stomach has a lot to do with *how you look, how you feel,* and *how you grow.* Eating **good foods** that are **good for you** is one of the best things you can do to help yourself be healthy, active and happy.

Your body is made to enjoy a variety of foods—especially nature's foods like fruits, vegetables, and whole grains which are used to make cereals, pastas, and breads. Eating a variety of *good foods* supplies the vitamins, nutrients, and calories you need for energy and growth.

## MAKING PLANS TO RUN AND EAT

It takes about 3-5 hours for most people to digest a meal. To avoid stomach upset and cramps, schedule the time you eat to fit in with the time you race or workout.

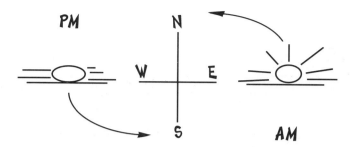

# EATING FOR MORNING RUNS

Running before breakfast is a great way to avoid stomach upset, and many runners have learned to do it successfully. You may only need a small glass of water before starting a warm-up and run.

If you plan a mid-morning exercise, eat a light breakfast of juice, toast, and/or a small bowl of cereal. Avoid eating eggs and meat, and don't drink large glasses of milk. These take a long time to digest and will slow you down or cause cramps.

# EATING FOR AFTERNOON RUNS

Eat lunch at least 3-4 hours before exercise. You'll be wise to avoid a lot of meat, cheese, milk, and peanut butter. Finish by having a piece of fresh fruit, and be sure to drink plenty of water.

# AFTER A RUN — RELOADING

Drink water after a run to replace fluids. At races, bring fruit, bagels, pretzels, or other healthy snacks to keep your energy up when the race is done.

Avoid junk food and soda before and after a race. Limit these even on the days you don't run. Let good food work for you. Let it help you in everything you do.

BE SURE TO VISIT THE HEALTHY SNACK BAR ON PAGES 138-9.

107

# ENERGY FOOD & AN ATHLETE'S BEST FRIEND

*There is energy food to help you feel good*
*the night before running a race.*
*It digests really fast and helps you to last*
*so you won't feel you're running in place.*

*Scientists tell us, as do great runners*
*that spaghetti is what you should eat.*
*Burgers and fries you'll avoid if you're wise*
*and choose pasta rather than meat.*

*Spaghetti and rice, potatoes and bread*
*store energy in food that tastes great.*
*In abundance they carry, for muscles that tarry,*
*a molecule called "carbohydrate".*

*Along with your pasta, eat veggies and fruit,*
*they're all natural and grow in the sun.*
*Packed full of energy, and vitamins plenty,*
*they make a great snack when you're done.*

*Water, too, is important for you*
*and perhaps most important of all.*
*It helps you stay fresh, so you'll do your best,*
*water can help you stand tall.*

*So remember to think, when you take a drink,*
*of safety while out in the sun.*
*Water bathes muscles, your skin and corpuscles,*
*it helps you have fun when you run.*

*After the race, be sure to replace*
*all the water you've lost by the end.*
*It's a great beverage, so give yourself leverage,*
*Water's An Athlete's Best Friend.*

**— TIM ERSON**

# Chapter 15

# Race Day

## Test Your
### S - T - R - E - T - C - H

**T**his is your **PARTY DAY!** A day to get up early, put on your favorite running clothes, and meet your friends and neighbors for the biggest event in town. Your training, preparation, and new skills are tested at races, so you'll want to feel your best. Races offer new challenges and experiences. Best of all, races offer you the chance to participate as an athlete.

# Entering a Race

Most events require that you fill out an application. Don't forget to fill out yours, and have it signed and sent in on time. Check where and when to pick up your race packet and number. Race applications are like party invitations and need a response.

At community races, fun runs, and walk-athons, you'll meet active people of all ages, sizes, and abilities. Some races offer t-shirts, refreshments, and other surprises too.

> *Races open you to new experiences and discoveries about yourself and the joy of participating as an athlete.*

# Your Race Plan

A day or two before the race, take some quiet time and think about the kind of race you want to run. If possible, discuss it with your coach. Do you want to run at an even pace? Do you want to start easy and do the second half fast? How fast do you want to run your first split? Will you try to lead or follow a pack? Will you run with someone you know?

# Countdown

Plan to arrive 45 minutes to an hour before a race starts. Give yourself time to warm up and take care of details.

### 30-40 minutes
- Find out where the race will start.
- Go to the bathroom early. Lines form later.
- Pin your race number on the *front* of your shirt.

### 20-30 minutes
Warm up with easy exercise and light jogging.

### 10-20 minutes
Continue stretching. Do 2 or 3 short, fast runs.

### 5-10 minutes

Take off your sweats, stay loose, and move toward the start.  Relax, and think about your plan.

When the race is called, listen for the official's final instructions.  Line up near people who will race at your speed.

## The Race

Have fun, and try to run the race you've planned.  Below are some other points to keep in mind.

- Don't use up all your energy at the start.

- Enjoy the company of other runners.  Be polite. Don't push or cut off other participants.

- Try to finish.  Stop only if you are sick or in extreme and unusual pain.

- When you approach the finish, watch for officials who will guide you.

## After the Race

- Drink water.  Jog or walk a few minutes to cool down.

- Don't let yourself get chilled.  Put on a clean, dry shirt.

- Show good sportsmanship.  Congratulate other runners. Cheer for those who are still finishing.

> *Races*
> *often bring out the best in us.*
> *From them,*
> *we learn about our training*
> *and can set new goals.*

# RACER'S CHECKLIST

## Signing up . . .

☐ Have your race application signed and sent in on time.

☐ Call the race information number in advance if you have questions or special needs.

☐ Know where and when to pick up your race packet and number.

## The Day Before . . .

☐ Make your final workout easy with stretching and light jogging. Feel *rested*, not sore, on race day.

☐ Enjoy a delicious pre-race meal.

☐ Pack your clothes and accessories the night before.

☐ Get a good night's sleep one and two nights before a race.

## Race Day . . .

☐ Drink water on hot days. Eat lightly, and avoid eating too much 3-5 hours before a race.

☐ Arrive early. (45-60 minutes)

☐ Start your Countdown.

Timothy E. Erson ©1993

## How did you do?

Write a note about your race on the back of your number and in your logbook. (see pages 257-263)

| Date | Event/Distance | Time | Weather Conditions |
|------|----------------|------|---------------------|
|      |                |      |  Temperature _____ ° |
| Comments _____ | | | |
| _____ | | | |
| _____ | | | |

## The Day After a Race . . .

Stretch, and take it easy.

Give yourself a break—

*You deserve it.*

**Chapter 16**

# INJURIES

## S-T-R-E-T-C-H
## Carefully

Injuries are likely to occur at some time in most athletic careers. You can do much to decrease your chances for injury and will appreciate the information in this chapter on:

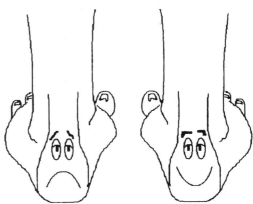

Areas of Injury
Caring for Injuries
Returning from an Injury
Preventing Injuries
Troubleshooter's Guide to Possible Causes

**Important Note:** All injuries have the potential to become more serious. The intention of this chapter is not to act as a substitute for medical care or advice. The information is only a guide to common athletic injuries in otherwise healthy individuals. If you become injured, or if you have special medical needs or circumstances, please consult and follow the advice of your doctor.

## Areas of Injury

Every sport has its own list of common injuries.  Usually, the body parts injured are the ones most often stressed.  In running and walking, most injuries occur in the legs and feet.

Muscles, tendons, ligaments, bones, blood vessels, nerves, and skin are the structures that make up our legs and feet.  Each has its own job, and each depends on the others to do its job effectively.  When one part hurts, all others are in some way affected.  Read the verses which follow, and see how it all makes sense.

Muscles are connected to tendons,
Tendons are connected to bones,
Bones are held in place by ligaments,
And that's what makes your joints.

Nerves are found in joints and muscles,
They sense the way your body moves,
Nerves tell muscles what to do,
And that's what moves your joints.

Let's not forget the blood vessels,
They carry to your legs food and oxygen,
The delivery is made through capillaries,
And it's all wrapped up in skin.

The best way to avoid an injury is to do all you can to prevent one.  Remember to:

1) warm up and cool down
2) dress properly
3) W-A-T-C-H  O-U-T !
4) alternate hard training days with easy
5) rest if you have pain.

## Caring for Injuries (3 R's)

If you do get injured or have unusual pain, follow the **3 R's**:

**R**est. Pain is the body's signal that something is wrong.

**R**eport it. Tell your coach, a qualified adult or medical person.

**R**eview your log. See what might be causing the pain.

## Using ICE to Care for Injuries

Many athletic injuries can be treated with ice. Sore muscles, tendons, and ligaments are often relieved by cold.

A cold pack with towels applied to healthy skin can relieve pain and decrease swelling. Many athletes use cold—10 minutes on, 10 minutes off, and 10 minutes on again—twice a day or as recommended. *Always follow the steps for injury care with the help and supervision of a responsible adult or medical professional.*

## Returning from an Injury

Some injuries take longer to heal than others. When you are pain free and ready to run or walk again, begin at slower speeds, shorter distances, and on flat surfaces. Take time to rebuild damaged tissue.

Depending on how much you've missed, it may be awhile before you return to your previous level of training. Muscles, tendons, ligaments, and bones all need to regain strength if you haven't been using them.

The good news about returning from an injury is that once you've been in shape, it doesn't take long to get back to it.

| 10 Factors that Lead to Injury or Illness | | Preventing Injuries |
|---|---|---|
| 1 | Overuse | Rest one or two days per week. Increase your distances slowly—no more than 5-10% a week. Alternate hard and easy days. |
| 2 | Hard Training Surfaces | Avoid training too much on concrete. (Concrete is 10 times harder than asphalt). Run on shock absorbing surfaces like dirt or grass. Use a well cushioned shoe. |
| 3 | Uneven Ground | Slow down, and watch your step on uneven or slippery surfaces. |
| 4 | Not Dressed Wisely or Improper Footwear | Dress Wisely. (See Ch. 3) |
| 5 | Weak Foot Muscles | Exercise feet by picking up marbles or scrunching a towel with your toes. Walk or run short distances barefoot on the beach or safe grass. Strong foot muscles prevent many foot injuries. |
| 6 | Dehydration/ Poor Nutrition/ Undigested Food | Drink plenty of water throughout the day to keep muscles hydrated. Proper nutrition is necessary for active tissue repair. |
| 7 | Poor Sleeping Habits | Get at least 8 hours sleep. Stay in rhythm with a regular sleep schedule. |
| 8 | Muscle Tightness | Do warm-ups and cool-downs to prevent muscle tightness and pulls. |
| 9 | Fast Downhill Running | Go easy when training downhill. Shock and muscle tension increase when you run down a hill fast. |
| 10 | Running with Injuries Not Yet Healed | Give injuries a chance to heal. Train comfortably, and avoid running with pain. |

Timothy E. Erson ©1993

| Troubleshooter's Guide Common Injuries | Possible Causes (Use with the *10 Factors* Chart) | | | | | | | | | |
|---|---|---|---|---|---|---|---|---|---|---|
| | 1 | 2 | 3 | 4 | 5 | 6 | 7 | 8 | 9 | 10 |
| Back pain | | ✳ | | | | | | ✳ | ✳ | |
| Blisters | | | | ✳ | | | | | | |
| Burnout & Chronic Fatigue | ✳ | | | | | ✳ | ✳ | | | ✳ |
| Foot pain | ✳ | ✳ | | ✳ | ✳ | | | | | ✳ |
| Heel pain | ✳ | ✳ | | ✳ | ✳ | | | ✳ | ✳ | ✳ |
| Hip pain | ✳ | ✳ | ✳ | | | | | ✳ | ✳ | ✳ |
| Hyperthermia (overheated) | | | | ✳ | | ✳ | ✳ | | | |
| Hypothermia (chilled) | | | | ✳ | | ✳ | ✳ | | | |
| Knee pain | ✳ | ✳ | ✳ | ✳ | | | | ✳ | ✳ | ✳ |
| Pulled muscles | ✳ | | | | | ✳ | | ✳ | ✳ | ✳ |
| Shin pain | ✳ | ✳ | | ✳ | ✳ | | | ✳ | ✳ | ✳ |
| Side pain | | | | | | ✳ | | | | |
| Sprained ankle | | | ✳ | ✳ | | | | | | ✳ |
| Stomach cramps | | | | | | ✳ | | | | |
| Sunburn | | | | ✳ | | | | | | |

Timothy E. Erson ©1993

## T**T**T  Staying in Shape When You're Injured

If an injury keeps you away from running or walking, consider other ways to exercise while you repair. Sometimes you can still swim, ride a bike, lift weights, or go shorter distances at slower speeds.

If an injury really has you "side-lined", and you can't exercise, use your healing time creatively to develop other areas in your life. Take time to read, write, draw, or play a musical instrument.

When I was 16, I broke my toe. My sister was learning to play the guitar and showed me a few chords. Though I was sad at not being able to run, I took interest in learning to play. Within a couple of weeks, my toe healed, and I went back to running. Today, I have enjoyed playing the guitar and running for many years.

**Chapter 17**

# Courageous Communities

S-T-R-E-T-C-H

Your Hope

**H**er feet were sore, and she was tired after a long day at work. It was December 1, 1955, in Montgomery, Alabama. The Christmas holidays were a little more than three weeks away. In her job as seamstress at a bustling, downtown department store, Rosa Parks had finished another busy day.

She left work and headed for the bus. It was not yet full, and she was happy to find a seat, even though it was toward the back, where the law at that time and place required African Americans to sit. The bus went along and filled with more passengers. Soon there were no seats left.

At one stop, a white man, also on his way home from work, boarded the bus. The driver demanded that Mrs. Parks give up her seat and move further back, where she'd have to stand. His words and action were rude and insensitive. Mrs. Parks knew in her heart that he was wrong—so she sat. Angrily, the driver got off the bus, called the police, and had her arrested.

Mrs. Rosa Parks

Mrs. Parks had never been arrested. To regard her as a criminal because she would not give up a bus seat that she had paid for was degrading and mean.

Her friends and neighbors were outraged. They rallied and talked about how to courageously end the suffering and humiliation that they and Rosa Parks had endured. How would they stand up to such cruel and unfair practices?

At 50,000 strong, the African American citizens of Montgomery could have reacted violently. Instead, their decision and determination was to respond peacefully. They would take positive action against a law that was hurtful and made no sense.

A decision was made to stop riding the buses. They would boycott them until all people were allowed to sit wherever they wanted, on a first come, first served basis.

When thousands of people at once stopped using the buses, the bus companies began to lose money. The people's commitment to walk long distances and travel less conveniently was having an effect. Still, the companies refused to let them sit where they wanted. The unfair law had not changed.

*One of the greatest stories of a Courageous Community is the story of that community's effort to right a wrong peacefully.*

Daily, for more than a year, in hot weather and in cold, in rain and in snow, African Americans in Montgomery chose to walk to work, to the store, or to visit friends and relatives, rather than take the bus.  By walking—by strengthening their bodies—they also strengthened their spirits and became courageous marchers—"pacers" for freedom.

Many people car pooled and took taxis, but most had to walk long distances.  They left their homes early in the morning, and did not return until late in the evening.  As their sense of purpose grew, their courage, confidence and self-esteem soared.  Martin Luther King, Jr., a leader and spokesperson for the citizens, summed up their feelings when he said, **In the long run, it is more honorable to walk in dignity than to ride in humiliation.**

Though their feet were tired, their hearts rejoiced, as they walked, and walked, and walked.  At meetings held in churches, they joined in song and prayer and supported one another with a spirit of courage.  So great was their courage that the whole world watched and sent reporters and journalists to see where such courage would lead.  Across America, in Europe, and around the world, people sent letters of support.  Some even made contributions to help the courageous cause.

Through courage, they gained the attention of the nation, the President, and the Supreme Court and changed an unfair law.  Eventually, the boycott ended.

Life in that city and in other places around the world continues to be changed every day by individuals and groups who dedicate themselves to such courage.  Courage, not to act violently and destroy, but *true courage, to move heroically and build a new and better world.*

> *In the long run, it is more honorable to walk in dignity than to ride in humiliation.*
> —M.L.K, Jr.

You never know when the strength of your body and depth of your feeling will be needed to help make the world a better place. One day, a courageous effort may need you. Keep listening. Keep training. Be part of courageous building.

Say, *Yes!* to what you believe in your heart is good
for people.

Say, *Yes!* to making the world's environment clean and safe
for *all* living things.

Say, *Yes!* to the chance for a good education. Be courageous,
and take that education
as far as you can.

And say, *Yes!*—giving **courage** and en**courage**ment to that
which strives for Wholeness and Peace
in YOUR Community and World.

### TᵀT

In every community, concerned citizens and groups work to make a better world. Many organize walkathons and fun runs to help fight disease, clean the environment, and support people in need. These events make us aware of what is being done every day to make our communities better.

If there is a concern that interests you, find out if there is a fun run or walkathon to support it. Consider joining that event.

*Courageous Pacers and Courageous Communities:*

Courageous enough to say **Yes!** to *improving their lives;*

Courageous enough to say **Yes!** to *improving their world.*

If you would like to learn more about Rosa Parks, Martin Luther King, Jr., and the Montgomery Bus Boycott, talk to your librarian. Read one of the many books written about them.

**Chapter 18**

# WINNERS

*I have learned that success is to be measured
not so much by the position that one has reached in life,
as by the obstacles which one has overcome
while trying to succeed.*

—Booker T. Washington

"Did you see the article in *Sports Illustrated*?" he asked.*

"What article?" I replied.

"The one about the Memphis Triathlon—I did it!"

I thought back to the time Tom lived in Brooklyn. I was one of several runners helping him train for the New York City Marathon. Tom, in his mid-20's, was blind and needed volunteers to guide him while training. Strong, fast, and fearless, Tom

Tom trains behind pick-up truck with partner David Marks.

*Photo by Angie Allison*

*"Seeing and Believing: A triathletes blindness doesn't impair his vision." Sports Illustrated, Mar 6,1989.

left many guides huffing and puffing as they tried to keep pace and protect him. It was possible to imagine Tom running—I'd seen him do it often—but how could he have done a triathlon? How could a person who is blind, swim and ride a bike? He often dreamed of doing one, but how would it be possible?

"How did you do it?" I asked. "How did you ride and steer a bike? Was it a two person bike?"

Tom gave me a big grin. "No," he said, "I rode by myself on a 10-speed. A friend rode ahead in the back of a pick-up truck and yelled directions through a bullhorn."

I was amazed. "Did you crash?" I asked.

"A few times," he said, and we both laughed.

"How did you do the swim?"

"Another friend helped me make a lane out of plastic tubing. We tied it to the back of a kayak, and I swam behind the boat."

> *It was clear—Tom had found a way to make his dream come true.*

This was exciting. What courage it must have taken to attempt and complete a triathlon. It was clear—Tom had found a way to make his dream come true.

## His Struggles

I was happy to see Tom that day. I had known him for several years and was aware of tremendous obstacles he had overcome. Active as a child, he lost his sight at age 19. Soon after, his father died. Needing to support himself and his mother, Tom looked everywhere for a job. He even called the governor, and finally one was found.

A few years later, his mother died, and Tom was on his own. Alone, he survived a difficult period in New York City. Eventually, he was accepted to Memphis State University and moved to Tennessee.

## A Second Triathlon Challenge

A year after he told me about his race, Tom and I talked on the phone. I mentioned that a triathlon was coming up in Corpus Christi. It included a 3/4 mile swim in Corpus Christi Bay, an 18 mile bike, and a 5 mile run. Tom had stayed in shape and wanted to give it a try.

"Will you help?" he asked.

"Yes", I replied.

Tom flew down two days before the race. He brought his swim lane but needed to borrow a bike. We adjusted my 10-speed and went to a deserted road to practice. A friend met us with his jeep. Tom and I figured out a system of calling out numbers to help him steer. As Tom mounted the bike, I hopped into the back of the jeep and faced him with a bullhorn.

Using the numbers 1-10, "5" indicated he was straight on course. The numbers "6, 7, or 8" meant he was veering to the left. If I called out "4, 3, or 2", it meant he was moving to the right. The number "1" or "10" signaled a dangerous edge. We practiced and made the system work. But could we keep it up for the 18 mile leg?

## Race Day

We were greeted with heat and humidity on race day. Bay waters, which are usually calm in the morning, had 1-2 foot waves rolling in. In the water, I saw cabbagehead jellyfish everywhere. They wouldn't have much of a sting, but they would be a nuisance.

A group of friends agreed to paddle a canoe, drive the jeep, and direct traffic at intersections. For safety, Tom suggested that he start 15 minutes after the other competitors. As he prepared for the swim, I wondered how well Tom and the rented canoe would do.

The gun sounded, and Tom waited as the other competitors dashed from shore. After 15 minutes, Tom followed the canoe into the water. Waves rushed quickly at the small boat, and it filled with water. Within a few yards, it swamped. Undeterred, Tom moved past the boat. A friend and I jumped in and swam on either side calling out to direct his path. Soon, a lifeguard joined us on a paddleboard.

It was not an easy swim. Waves rolled at us, and Tom never knew when they would hit. Even with our warnings, it was difficult for him to time his breaths, and he swallowed a lot of water. Tom coughed several times as we headed to the turn around. Tossed by waves, and touched by jellyfish, Tom persevered and worked to remain calm. Occasionally, he stopped to tread water and clear his lungs. Through it, he kept his humor and said, "I feel like I'm in a washing machine."

We were happy when the swim was over and made our way to the transition area to begin the bike. On the road, Tom mounted my 10-speed. Daringly, he followed the jeep he could not see, while I called out numbers to guide him. Pedaling hard, he reached speeds of 20-22 miles an hour on the flat and winding road.

At nine miles, we stopped for water. No sooner had we stopped when Tom was ready to get back on and finish the final nine. In the last 200 yards, the road narrowed and snaked down a hill. Twice, Tom crashed into the curb but was able to catch himself. Finally, we made it to the end.

Tom got off the bike and was ready to run as I climbed out of the jeep. This 5 mile leg would be easy compared to everything he had just done. Together, we ran side by side as we had done years before while training and racing in New York.

With two miles to go, Tom began to catch competitors who had started ahead of him. Near the end, athletes and spectators spotted him and yelled, "Here comes Tom. Look, he made it!" As he crossed the line, there was a great cheer.

Tom was a hero that day. Modestly, and with a big grin, he proved that *what a person believes, he really can achieve if he works hard to find the answers.*

At the awards ceremony, Tom's name was picked in a raffle. He won a dinner for two and invited me to join him. As we reminisced, I realized that what he had done with a dream, and the help of friends, was one of the greatest efforts I'd ever seen in sports.

## Corpus Christi Caller Times

| One Dollar | More than 217,800 Sunday readers | April 22, 1990 |
| --- | --- | --- |

### Triathlete is victor against adversity

**By Chuck DeCarbo**

STAFF WRITER

During the three-quarter mile swim in choppy Corpus Christi Bay, triathlete

"Now, I take things for what they are, not for what they look like."

## WHAT MAKES SOMEBODY A WINNER ?

Medals, trophies, and awards don't declare the only winners in a race. *Winning is a feeling that comes from doing your very best.* Everyone has the chance to become a winner in a race because everyone has the chance to do their best. Tom O'Connor is a winner because he uses his energy, imagination, and determination to compete and overcome obstacles.

### Author's Note

Tom wins at more than races and triathlons. He also:

* ice-skates
* cooks gourmet meals
* performs judo and karate
* rides horses
* canoe races
* sky dives

* barefoot waterskis
* has run for city council
* has been recognized by the City of Memphis for helping disabled people in sports.

133

## Chapter 19

# Shows to Give Your Shoes Time to Rest
## Featuring: The Healthy Snack Bar

## Running Videos

***Aesop's Fables: The Tortoise and the Hare and Other Tales.*** 1981.

This animated video includes 9 of Aesop's best loved animal tales. The race between the tortoise and the hare is every bit as exciting as when he first told it more than 2,500 years ago. I loved this one.

***Animalympics.*** 1981.

The first modern animalympic games is presented in the style of a

network sports extravaganza. ZOO-TV calls it "the beast in sports." Animated.

***Billie.*** 1965.

A comedy starring Patty Duke. Set in the 1960's, Billie causes controversy when the coach tries to recruit her for the boy's track team.

***Chariots of Fire.*** 1981.

A running movie that won an Oscar for Best Picture. The story of two British athletes and their quests to compete in the 1924 Olympics. A see-it-again movie.

***The Jesse Owens Story.*** 1984.

A sensitive portrait of the man who won four gold medals at the Berlin Olympics and overcame poverty and racial injustice. The story of a hero. A two part video.

***Jim Thorpe—All American.*** 1951.

The story of Native American Jim Thorpe. Winner of the Pentathlon and Decathlon in the 1912 Olympics, Thorpe has been called "the greatest athlete that ever lived". Stars Burt Lancaster.

***The Lonliest Runner.*** 1976.

A story of courage and fear, produced and directed by Michael Landon. A young adolescent runs in order to cope with a difficult personal and family matter.

***An Olympic Fable: Run For Life.*** 1983.

A children's film set in ancient Greece. It is the story of a friend's trust and another's courage to save his friend's life. Animated.

***On the Edge.*** 1986.

Bruce Dern plays a 44-year-old athlete unfairly banned from competition. He comes back after 20 years to race the grueling 14.2 mile Cielo-Sea race in Northern California. Seeing the race will have you *on the edge* of your seat.

***Running Brave.*** 1983.

The true story of Billy Mills, a Native American who grew up on a South Dakota reservation. Mills was the 10,000 meter gold medalist at the 1964 Olympics in Tokyo. Inspiring. Stars Robby Benson.

***A Shining Season.*** 1979.

The courageous story of young Olympic hopeful, John Baker, who battles cancer and coaches a kids' running team. Stars Timothy Bottoms.

***The Terry Fox Story.*** 1983.

Terry Fox loses his leg to cancer but finds the courage to pursue his dream—a run across Canada in a "Marathon of Hope". Inspiring portrait of a hero.

***Wilma.*** 1977.

Based on Wilma Rudolf's autobiography. Wilma overcomes poverty and disease to triumph with three gold medals at the Olympics in Rome.

***The World's Greatest Athlete.*** 1973.
A Disney comedy about a small college's attempt to solve its athletic woes by recruiting a Tarzan-like character named Nanu.

## Olympic Documentaries

There are many Olympic Documentaries. A few are mentioned here. Check the directory at your local video store for more.

**Barcelona** (1992)
**Olympic Gold Medal Winners** (1989)
**Gold Medal Champions** (1988)
**Seoul Olympic Track and Field: Men and Women** (1988)
**The Supermilers** (BBC film, 1986)
**16 Days to Glory** (1984)

**The Olympiad Series.** Produced and directed by Bud Greenspan.
Includes 22 videos filled with stories from the Olympics. The series is well made and worth finding. Some of my favorite titles include:

> **The African Runners**
> **The Australians**
> **The Decathlon**
> **The 800 Meters**
> **The Fastest Men in the World**
> **The 1500 Meters**
> **The Incredible Five**
> **Jesse Owens Returns to Berlin**
> **The Magnificent Ones**
> **The Marathon**
> **An Olympic Symphony**
> **The Rare Ones**
> **They Didn't Have a Chance**
> **Women Gold-Medal Winners**

## Other Winning Videos

***Breaking Away.*** 1979.
Four friends have trouble finding direction after graduating high school. A bicycle race helps give their lives purpose.

***The Long Walk Home.*** 1990.
A powerful story of two women during the days of the Montgomery Bus Boycott. Stars Whoopi Goldberg and Sissy Spacek.

***Stand and Deliver.*** 1988.
East L.A. teens prepare for an Advanced Placement Calculus Exam. A true and inspiring story of teamwork in the classroom. Stars James Olmos & Lou Diamond Phillips.

## Special Emphasis Videos

***Reach for Fitness.*** 1986. 40 min.
Richard Simmons' aerobic workout for children and adults who use wheelchairs. Includes helpful information on diet.

***Preparing to Meet . . . The Marathon Challenge.*** 1984.
A British documentary follows the progress of eight ordinary people training to do an extraordinary event—their first marathon.

# THE HEALTHY

**Fresh Fruit BOWL**

Tropical   Citrus   Apples
Melons   Berries

**TOASTED SEEDS:**

PUMPKIN
SUNFLOWER

Use a Juice Extractor to:

**COMBINE
ANY OR
ALL**

{ **CARROTS
CELERY
APPLES** }

## DRINKS

### FRUIT SHAKES

Recipe: Mix any amount of
the following in a blender:
1. Soy milk/Rice milk/Plain
   Yogurt
2. fruit juice—O. J. or apple
3. banana, plus any other
   fresh fruit (no seeds)

Mmmm…delicious!

### FRUIT JUICES

Apple
Grapefruit
Peach
Orange
& the exotic ones
from your grocery
store

### QUENCHERS

Carbonated water
with natural fruit
flavors
Homemade lemonade
(low sugar)
Spritzer—club soda &
fruit juice
Water—An Athlete's
Best Friend

# SNACK BAR

**Other Snacks:**
Applesauce
Pretzels
Raisins or Fresh Fruit
Bread sticks
Peanut butter on celery
No or low sugar cereal with fruit juice
Frozen Fruit Juice Pops (homemade)
Rice cakes with fruit jelly (no sugar)
Oven-baked potato & corn chips

AIR-POPPED
POPCORN
(NO BUTTER, PLEASE)
(LOW SALT)

NEW!
Fruit-Juice-Sweetened
Cookies

CRUNCHY
VEGETABLES

CARROTS    CELERY
BROCCOLI    CUCUMBERS
CAULIFLOWER

**Chapter 20**

# The Finals

*I tear right down the straightaway*
*No runners are around.*
*My energy food is working*
*Every step I'm gaining ground.*
*I round the curve with breakneck speed*
*Oh what a glorious day.*
*Til I see the runners up the track*
*Coming the other way.*

*—author unknown*

**D**o you have a favorite training/racing story or poem?  Send us a copy with your name, address, and age.  We'll contact you if we decide to use it in a future publication.

Our address:     Stories & Poems
                 PRO-ACTIV Publications
                 P. O. Box 331186
                 Corpus Christi, TX 78463-1186

## You've Made it to the Finals

In this chapter, we'll see how much you've learned, and you'll have a chance to earn a free S-T-R-E-T-C-H Training Tips magnet. You'll also learn a way to be *pro-active* about kids running.

## Problem Solving

Fill in the missing letters of the words below. Then, use the underlined letters to answer the question which follows.

__ - T - __ - E - T - C - H

L - I - F - __

__ - __ - S - Y

W - __ - T - __ - H    O - U - T!

Where do runners and walkers celebrate?

___ ___    ___ ___ ___ ___ ___

## Math Miles

> 1 mile = 5,280 feet
>
> 1 yard = 3 feet

1. On a rural road, the distance between telephone
   poles is 330 feet.  How many poles would
   you have to pass to run one mile?

   **Answer:** _____

2. A soccer field is 70 yards long and 40 yards wide.  About
   how many laps would you have to run for one mile?

   **Answer:** _____

3. a.  In baseball, the distance between each base is 90 feet.
   If a person hits a home run, how many feet will they
   have to run?

   **Answer:** _____

   b.  How many home runs must a player hit
   to log one mile around the bases?

   **Answer:** _____

### BONUS:

Hank Aaron hit 755 home runs in the major leagues.
How many miles did Hank Aaron run to set that record?

**Answer:** _____

## BE PROACTIVE ABOUT KIDS RUNNING

On page 147 is a letter to send to the Road Runners Club of America. This non-profit organization does much for runners and walkers.  It promotes our sport nationwide but depends on local athletes to share their needs and concerns.

I am concerned that entry fees at some races are too high for children, groups of children, and families who like to race often.  In the letter,  I express my concern and hope you will join me.  Let's alert race directors about the need to make our sport more available to kids.

**Here's your chance to earn a prize.** Do the crossword puzzle, and answer the questions on page 146. When you've finished, tear it out, and send it to us with your name and address. (Photocopies are not accepted.) We will send you a free S-T-R-E-T-C-H Training Tips magnet. One prize per reader. Good luck!

## Across

1) A _____ pin holds the number on your shirt.
3) _____ O-U-T
7) what it takes to be a kid
9) 5280 ft.
10) _____ for LIFE
11) once around the track
12) training buddies
14) a canine partner
15) Injuries take time to _____ .
16) __ - _____ and shorts
19) Milers combine speed and _____ .
21) Running and walking are _____ .
22) WATCH- ____
23) _____ partners
24) _____ Rudolph
28) strengthening guide (one word)
29) a record of a journey
31) spaghetti and _____, potatoes and bread
33) anchor ____
34) "with oxygen"
35) _____'s Corner

## Down

1) _____ Time Review
2) 3200 meters = ___ miles
3) the _____ Brothers
4) winner of Aesop's race
5) keeps your head warm
6) Wilma's coach, Ed _____
7) Pasta is a complex _____ .
8) runner's party
10) marathoner's food
12) macaroni, linguini, wagon wheels
13) Five _____ exercises for arms and trunk
17) _____ Parks
18) Logbook & _____
20) _____ & walking
21) _____ help motivate you
24) run or _____
25) Kilo_____
26) a course around an area
27) an athlete's best friend
30) relieves sore muscles
32) On your mark, get set, ___!

# CROSSWORD PUZZLE

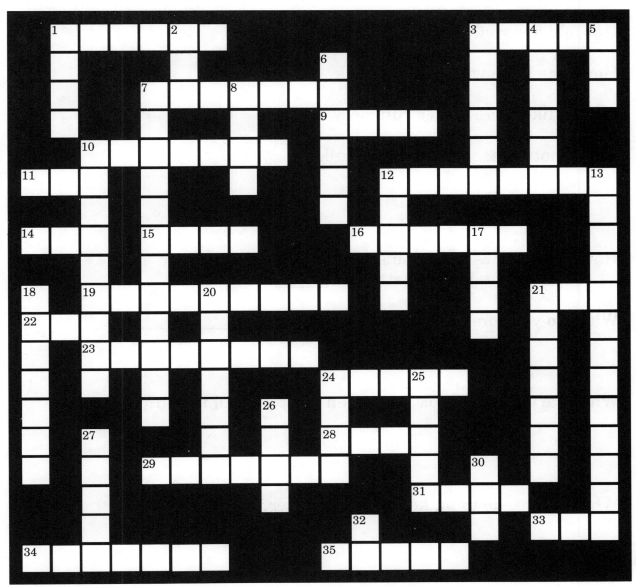

**Bonus Question:** About how many miles did Hank Aaron run by hitting 755 Home Runs? (see p. 143)

Name _____

Address _____

City/State/Zip _____

No photocopies accepted. Please send this page.

Timothy E. Erson ©1993

145

Please take time to answer the questions below. Your ideas are important to us and will help us give kids better information in the future.

How old are you? _____

How long have you had this book? _____

Do you like to (circle one) run or walk ?

What motivates you to run or walk?

How many times have you entered a race, fun run, or walkathon in the last year? _____

What do you consider your best distance? _____

What parts of this book have been most helpful to you?

What can we do to make this book better?

Please send to:  PRO-ACTIV Publications
                 P. O. Box 331186
                 Corpus Christi, Texas 78463-1186

Thanks!  Please allow 3-4 weeks for delivery of your prize.

Name _____

Address _____

City, State, Zip _____

Date _____

President, Road Runners Club of America
National Office
1150 S. Washington St., Suite 250
Alexandria, VA  22314

Dear RRCA President,

Thanks for the support you and your organization give to running, walking, and racing in communities nationwide.  Without you, many local clubs, races, and fun runs would not exist.

I am _____ years old and enjoy (circle one) running/walking because:

1) _____

2) _____

3) _____ .

I'm writing in support of children's running and to encourage community race directors to make races affordable to children, children's groups, and families.  Directors who want to raise money should do so from adult and business supporters.  Most kids don't earn a lot of money.

Please help race directors understand that lower fees for kids will attract more kids, and more kids will bring more adults.  More adults will make happier sponsors, and they in turn will support races more generously.

Thanks to the many race directors who invite and encourage kids to participate.  Let's all work together to make America's future road racing the best it can be.

Sincerely,

_____
Sign your name here.

P. S.

☐ I belong to the _____ Running Club.

☐ I do not belong to a running club.  Please send me information about clubs in my area.  Thanks.

# Epilogue

# S - T - R - E - T - C - H
# Over Hurdles
# with L I F E

In the introduction, I wrote that it takes courage to be a kid these days—courage to move your life positively and confidently. Today's world is challenging. There is opportunity to improve your life, but trying to figure out what's best isn't always easy. To live courageously means to grow and to reach for your best self.

Continue to enjoy running and walking. Find ways to get involved with clubs, events, and programs near you. Running and walking are life skills that promote courageous, active and happy living. They help you improve not only as an athlete but in other areas of life.

Life isn't always easy. There are victories every day, but sometimes there are setbacks. Sometimes hurdles pop up, and you get discouraged. Although it can be hard, **never give up.** Getting beyond hurdles and on track toward worthwhile goals is what makes you a winner.

There's a formula to remember which builds courage and can help you when you face hurdles. It's easy to learn, and *sticking with it works.* And, wouldn't you know it, all you have to do is remember one simple word:

# L - I - F - E

**L = *Listen to your heart.*** Spend time away from TV, music, and the news. Go for a quiet run or walk. Get to know *you*.

**I = *Invest in your community.*** Volunteer. Do something nice for someone.

**F = *Fortify your body.*** Strengthen it with exercise, and eat healthy food.

**E = *Educate your mind.*** Read, write, and learn new skills. Add positive thoughts and new ideas.

*L-I-F-E:* It'll give you a new perspective.

Timothy E. Erson ©1993

151

Do you know someone who would like to receive the *Courageous Pacers* book as a gift?

# GIFT IDEA

| Gift from: | Please send gift book to: |
|---|---|
| Name _____ | Name _____ |
| Address _____ | Address _____ |
| City _____ | City _____ |
| State _____ Zip _____ | State _____ Zip _____ |
| Gift card message: _____ |
| _____ |

| # of copies | Price | Subtotal |
|---|---|---|
| | $18.95 | |
| S & H | $2.00/bk (1-3 bks) $1.00 ea. add. bk | |
| Tax 7 3/4 % in TX | | |
| Total | | |

Send a check or money order to:
**PRO-ACTIV Publications**
**P.O. Box 331186**
**Corpus Christi, TX 78463-1186**

---

Do you know someone who would like to receive the *Courageous Pacers* book as a gift?

# GIFT IDEA

| Gift from: | Please send gift book to: |
|---|---|
| Name _____ | Name _____ |
| Address _____ | Address _____ |
| City _____ | City _____ |
| State _____ Zip _____ | State _____ Zip _____ |
| Gift card message: _____ |
| _____ |

| # of copies | Price | Subtotal |
|---|---|---|
| | $18.95 | |
| S & H | $2.00/bk (1-3 bks) $1.00 ea. add. bk | |
| Tax 7 3/4 % in TX | | |
| Total | | |

Send a check or money order to:
**PRO-ACTIV Publications**
**P.O. Box 331186**
**Corpus Christi, TX 78463-1186**

---

Do you know someone who would like to receive the *Courageous Pacers* book as a gift?

# GIFT IDEA

| Gift from: | Please send gift book to: |
|---|---|
| Name _____ | Name _____ |
| Address _____ | Address _____ |
| City _____ | City _____ |
| State _____ Zip _____ | State _____ Zip _____ |
| Gift card message: _____ |
| _____ |

| # of copies | Price | Subtotal |
|---|---|---|
| | $18.95 | |
| S & H | $2.00/bk (1-3 bks) $1.00 ea. add. bk | |
| Tax 7 3/4 % in TX | | |
| Total | | |

Send a check or money order to:
**PRO-ACTIV Publications**
**P.O. Box 331186**
**Corpus Christi, TX 78463-1186**

# Logbook & Journal

**SAMPLE LOG PAGE**

**Training Goal:** This week I will ___run 15 miles,___ ___and enter a 5K race.___ .

HUH!

| | Date | Distance or Time | Training Notes | Weather Conditions | Strengthening |
|---|---|---|---|---|---|
| M O N | 3/16 | 2 | Easy pace. Ran park loop. body weight 112 | T = 57° | 2 x 10 reps 4 lbs. L-I-F-T |
| T U E | 3/17 | 4 | Fartlek run in park—slight pain in left hamstring on final downhill. | Windy Sun (Cloudy) Rain Snow  Indoor  T = Temperature | |
| W E D | 3/18 | 1 | Light stretching. Walked one mile. No pain in left leg. | T = 63° | 2 x 10 reps L-I-F-T |
| T H R | 3/19 | 3 | Ran neighborhood loop with friend. Finished with 4 x 100 yd uphill runs. | T = 67° | |
| F R I | 3/20 | 1 | Stretched and jogged easy 1 mile | T = 67° | Basketball shooting 30 minutes |
| S A T | 3/21 | 4 | Race—Save Our Park 5K warm-up and cool-down See race log | T = 70° | |
| S U N | 3/22 | 0 | Rest | T = ___° | Dug vegetable garden. |

| 15 | **Distance or time this week** |
|---|---|
| + 73 | all other weeks |
| = 88 | New TOTAL |

*Other Activities I Did This Week:*

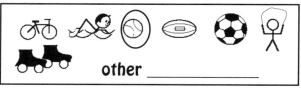

**other** _____

S T R E T C H

Timothy E. Erson ©1993

# Training Courses

List your training courses here.  Give each a name or number.

| Name or Number | Course Description | Distance |
|---|---|---|
| | | |
| | | |
| | | |
| | | |
| | | |
| | | |
| | | |

**LOG PAGE**

**Training Goal:** This week I will ___try to___
___run 22 laps in P.E.___

**HUH!**

| | Date | Distance or Time | Training Notes | Weather Conditions | Strengthening |
|---|---|---|---|---|---|
| MON | Nov. 6, 95. | 12 laps | I felt good because it was raining and we had no playground | T = 70° | None |
| TUE | | | | T = ___° | |
| WED | | | | T = ___° | |
| THR | | | | T = ___° | |
| FRI | | | | T = ___° | |
| SAT | | | | T = ___° | |
| SUN | | | | T = ___° | |

☐ **Distance or time this week**

+ ☐ all other weeks

= ☐ New TOTAL

*Other Activities I Did This Week:*

**other** _____

**S T R E T C H**

# JOURNAL

*A journey of a thousand miles begins with one step.*
—Lao-Tzu

# LOG PAGE

**Training Goal:** This week I will _____

_____

HUH!

| | Date | Distance or Time | Training Notes | Weather Conditions | Strengthening |
|---|---|---|---|---|---|
| MON | | | | T = _____ ° | |
| TUE | | | | T = _____ ° | |
| WED | | | | T = _____ ° | |
| THR | | | | T = _____ ° | |
| FRI | | | | T = _____ ° | |
| SAT | | | | T = _____ ° | |
| SUN | | | | T = _____ ° | |

Timothy E. Erson ©1993

[ ] **Distance or time this week**

+ [ ] all other weeks

= [ ] New TOTAL

*Other Activities I Did This Week:*

other _____

158

S-T-R-E-T-C-H

# JOURNAL

*Nothing is particularly hard if you divide it into small jobs.*
—Henry Ford

_____

_____

_____

_____

_____

_____

_____

_____

_____

_____

_____

_____

_____

_____

_____

_____

_____

_____

_____

_____

_____

_____

## LOG PAGE

**Training Goal:** This week I will _____

_____

HUH!

| | Date | Distance or Time | Training Notes | Weather Conditions | Strengthening |
|---|---|---|---|---|---|
| MON | | | | T = _____ ° | |
| TUE | | | | T = _____ ° | |
| WED | | | | T = _____ ° | |
| THR | | | | T = _____ ° | |
| FRI | | | | T = _____ ° | |
| SAT | | | | T = _____ ° | |
| SUN | | | | T = _____ ° | |

Timothy E. Erson ©1993

☐ **Distance or time this week**

**+** ☐ all other weeks

**=** ☐ New TOTAL

*Other Activities I Did This Week:*

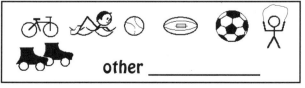

other _____

S  T  R  E  T  C  H

# JOURNAL

*We run, not because we think it is doing us good, but because we enjoy it and cannot help ourselves.  It also does us good because it helps us do other things better.*

—Roger Bannister

_____

_____

_____

_____

_____

_____

_____

_____

_____

_____

_____

_____

_____

_____

_____

_____

_____

**LOG PAGE**

**Training Goal:** This week I will _____

_____

HUH!

| | Date | Distance or Time | Training Notes | Weather Conditions | Strengthening |
|---|---|---|---|---|---|
| **MON** | | | | T = _____ ° | |
| **TUE** | | | | T = _____ ° | |
| **WED** | | | | T = _____ ° | |
| **THR** | | | | T = _____ ° | |
| **FRI** | | | | T = _____ ° | |
| **SAT** | | | | T = _____ ° | |
| **SUN** | | | | T = _____ ° | |

Timothy E. Erson ©1993

[ ] **Distance or time this week**

+ [ ] all other weeks

= [ ] New TOTAL

*Other Activities I Did This Week:*

**other** _____

S T R E T C H

# JOURNAL

*In the long run people hit only what they aim at.*
*Therefore . . . they had better aim at something high.*
—Henry David Thoreau

**LOG PAGE**

**Training Goal:** This week I will _____

_____

HUH!

| | Date | Distance or Time | Training Notes | Weather Conditions | Strengthening |
|---|---|---|---|---|---|
| MON | | | | T = _____ ° | |
| TUE | | | | T = _____ ° | |
| WED | | | | T = _____ ° | |
| THR | | | | T = _____ ° | |
| FRI | | | | T = _____ ° | |
| SAT | | | | T = _____ ° | |
| SUN | | | | T = _____ ° | |

Timothy E. Erson ©1993

☐ **Distance or time this week**

+ ☐ all other weeks

= ☐ New TOTAL

*Other Activities I Did This Week:*

**other** _____

164

S T R E T C H

# JOURNAL

*Failure is not falling down—it's staying down.*

—Claude Axel

_____

_____

_____

_____

_____

_____

_____

_____

_____

_____

_____

_____

_____

_____

_____

_____

_____

_____

_____

_____

_____

**LOG PAGE**

**Training Goal:** This week I will _____

_____

HUH!

| | Date | Distance or Time | Training Notes | Weather Conditions | Strengthening |
|---|------|------------------|----------------|--------------------|---------------|
| MON | | | | T = _____ ° | |
| TUE | | | | T = _____ ° | |
| WED | | | | T = _____ ° | |
| THR | | | | T = _____ ° | |
| FRI | | | | T = _____ ° | |
| SAT | | | | T = _____ ° | |
| SUN | | | | T = _____ ° | |

Timothy E. Erson ©1993

[ ] **Distance or time this week**

+ [ ] all other weeks

= [ ] New TOTAL

*Other Activities I Did This Week:*

other _____

S T R E T C H

# JOURNAL

*In any moment of decision, the best thing you can do is the right thing. The worst thing you can do is nothing.*
—Theodore Roosevelt

_____

_____

_____

_____

_____

_____

_____

_____

_____

_____

_____

_____

_____

_____

_____

_____

_____

_____

_____

## LOG PAGE

**Training Goal:** This week I will _____

_____

**Huh!**

| | Date | Distance or Time | Training Notes | Weather Conditions | Strengthening |
|---|---|---|---|---|---|
| **M O N** | | | | T = _____ ° | |
| **T U E** | | | | T = _____ ° | |
| **W E D** | | | | T = _____ ° | |
| **T H R** | | | | T = _____ ° | |
| **F R I** | | | | T = _____ ° | |
| **S A T** | | | | T = _____ ° | |
| **S U N** | | | | T = _____ ° | |

Timothy E. Erson ©1993

☐ **Distance or time this week**

+ ☐ all other weeks

= ☐ New TOTAL

*Other Activities I Did This Week:*

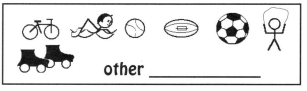

other _____

S - T - R - E - T - C - H

# JOURNAL

*Life is either a daring adventure or nothing.*
—Helen Keller

_____

_____

_____

_____

_____

_____

_____

_____

_____

_____

_____

_____

_____

_____

_____

_____

_____

_____

_____

_____

**Training Goal:** This week I will _____

_____

HUH!

| | Date | Distance or Time | Training Notes | Weather Conditions | Strengthening |
|---|---|---|---|---|---|
| **MON** | | | | T = _____ ° | |
| **TUE** | | | | T = _____ ° | |
| **WED** | | | | T = _____ ° | |
| **THR** | | | | T = _____ ° | |
| **FRI** | | | | T = _____ ° | |
| **SAT** | | | | T = _____ ° | |
| **SUN** | | | | T = _____ ° | |

☐ **Distance or time this week**

+ ☐ all other weeks

= ☐ New TOTAL

*Other Activities I Did This Week:*

other _____

S T R E T C H

170

Timothy E. Erson ©1993

# JOURNAL

*You can amaze your body, if you just keep telling yourself,*
*I can do it, I can do it, I can do it.*
— Jon Erickson

**Training Goal:** This week I will _____

_____

*HuH!*

| Date | Distance or Time | Training Notes | Weather Conditions | Strengthening |
|---|---|---|---|---|
| **MON** | | | T = _____ ° | |
| **TUE** | | | T = _____ ° | |
| **WED** | | | T = _____ ° | |
| **THR** | | | T = _____ ° | |
| **FRI** | | | T = _____ ° | |
| **SAT** | | | T = _____ ° | |
| **SUN** | | | T = _____ ° | |

Timothy E. Erson ©1993

☐ **Distance or time this week**

+ ☐  all other weeks

= ☐  New TOTAL

*Other Activities I Did This Week:*

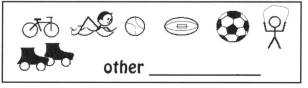

other _____

S T R E T C H

# JOURNAL

*The future belongs to those who believe
in the beauty of their dreams.*
—Eleanor Roosevelt

# LOG PAGE

**Training Goal:** This week I will _____

_____

HUH!

| Date | Distance or Time | Training Notes | Weather Conditions | Strengthening |
|---|---|---|---|---|
| **MON** | | | T = _____ ° | |
| **TUE** | | | T = _____ ° | |
| **WED** | | | T = _____ ° | |
| **THR** | | | T = _____ ° | |
| **FRI** | | | T = _____ ° | |
| **SAT** | | | T = _____ ° | |
| **SUN** | | | T = _____ ° | |

Timothy E. Erson ©1993

☐ **Distance or time this week**

+ ☐ all other weeks

= ☐ New TOTAL

*Other Activities I Did This Week:*

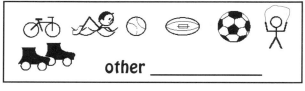

**other** _____

174

S · T · R · E · T · C · H

# JOURNAL

*Confidence doesn't come out of nowhere. It is a result of something. . . . hours, days, weeks and years of constant work and dedication.*

—Roger Staubach

# LOG PAGE

**Training Goal:** This week I will _____

_____

*HUH!*

| Date | Distance or Time | Training Notes | Weather Conditions | Strengthening |
|------|------------------|----------------|---------------------|---------------|
| **MON** | | | T = _____° | |
| **TUE** | | | T = _____° | |
| **WED** | | | T = _____° | |
| **THR** | | | T = _____° | |
| **FRI** | | | T = _____° | |
| **SAT** | | | T = _____° | |
| **SUN** | | | T = _____° | |

Timothy E. Erson ©1993

☐  **Distance or time this week**

+ ☐  all other weeks

= ☐  New TOTAL

*Other Activities I Did This Week:*

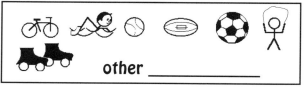

**other** _____

S T R E T C H

# JOURNAL

*I do the very best I know how—the very best I can;
and I mean to keep on doing so until the end.*
—Abraham Lincoln

## LOG PAGE

**Training Goal:** This week I will _____

_____

| | Date | Distance or Time | Training Notes | Weather Conditions | HUH! Strengthening |
|---|---|---|---|---|---|
| MON | | | | T = _____ ° | |
| TUE | | | | T = _____ ° | |
| WED | | | | T = _____ ° | |
| THR | | | | T = _____ ° | |
| FRI | | | | T = _____ ° | |
| SAT | | | | T = _____ ° | |
| SUN | | | | T = _____ ° | |

Timothy E. Erson ©1993

[ ] **Distance or time this week**

+ [ ] all other weeks

= [ ] New TOTAL

*Other Activities I Did This Week:*

other _____

S T R E T C H

# JOURNAL

*Plodding wins the race.*
—Aesop

# LOG PAGE

**Training Goal:** This week I will _____

_____

HUH!

| Date | Distance or Time | Training Notes | Weather Conditions | Strengthening |
|------|------------------|----------------|--------------------|---------------|
| **MON** | | | T = _____ ° | |
| **TUE** | | | T = _____ ° | |
| **WED** | | | T = _____ ° | |
| **THR** | | | T = _____ ° | |
| **FRI** | | | T = _____ ° | |
| **SAT** | | | T = _____ ° | |
| **SUN** | | | T = _____ ° | |

☐ **Distance or time this week**

+ ☐ all other weeks

= ☐ New TOTAL

*Other Activities I Did This Week:*

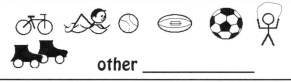

other _____

S  T  R  E  T  C  H

180

Timothy E. Erson ©1993

# JOURNAL

*Keep yourself clean and bright. You are the window through which you must see the world.*
—George Bernard Shaw

**LOG PAGE**

**Training Goal:** This week I will _____

_____

| | Date | Distance or Time | Training Notes | Weather Conditions | Strengthening |
|---|---|---|---|---|---|
| MON | | | | T = _____ ° | |
| TUE | | | | T = _____ ° | |
| WED | | | | T = _____ ° | |
| THR | | | | T = _____ ° | |
| FRI | | | | T = _____ ° | |
| SAT | | | | T = _____ ° | |
| SUN | | | | T = _____ ° | |

HUH!

Timothy E. Erson ©1993

☐ **Distance or time this week**

+ ☐ all other weeks

= ☐ New TOTAL

*Other Activities I Did This Week:*

other _____

S T R E T C H

# JOURNAL

*There is a bond among athletes of every race, religion, and color, that transcends all prejudice.*
—Jesse Owens

_____

_____

_____

_____

_____

_____

_____

_____

_____

_____

_____

_____

_____

_____

_____

_____

_____

_____

_____

**LOG PAGE**

**Training Goal:** This week I will _____

_____

HUH!

| | Date | Distance or Time | Training Notes | Weather Conditions | Strengthening |
|---|---|---|---|---|---|
| **MON** | | | | T = _____ ° | |
| **TUE** | | | | T = _____ ° | |
| **WED** | | | | T = _____ ° | |
| **THR** | | | | T = _____ ° | |
| **FRI** | | | | T = _____ ° | |
| **SAT** | | | | T = _____ ° | |
| **SUN** | | | | T = _____ ° | |

Timothy E. Erson ©1993

[ ] **Distance or time this week**

+ [ ] all other weeks

= [ ] New TOTAL

*Other Activities I Did This Week:*

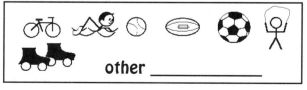

other _____

S-T-R-E-T-C-H

# JOURNAL

> *Heroism means being great in what every human can be great in — simply, doing the best you can.*
> —Soren Kierkegaard

_____

_____

_____

_____

_____

_____

_____

_____

_____

_____

_____

_____

_____

_____

_____

_____

_____

_____

_____

**LOG PAGE**

**Training Goal:** This week I will _____

_____

| | Date | Distance or Time | Training Notes | Weather Conditions | Strengthening HUH! |
|---|---|---|---|---|---|
| **MON** | | | | T = ____ ° | |
| **TUE** | | | | T = ____ ° | |
| **WED** | | | | T = ____ ° | |
| **THR** | | | | T = ____ ° | |
| **FRI** | | | | T = ____ ° | |
| **SAT** | | | | T = ____ ° | |
| **SUN** | | | | T = ____ ° | |

Timothy E. Erson ©1993

[ ] **Distance or time this week**

+ [ ] all other weeks

= [ ] New TOTAL

*Other Activities I Did This Week:*

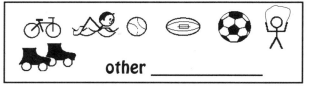

other _____

S—T—R—E—T—C—H

# JOURNAL

*Concentrate on one thing at a time and rule out all outside influences that don't have any real bearing on the task at hand.*

—Marty Liquori

# LOG PAGE

**Training Goal:** This week I will _____

_____

**HUH!**

| | Date | Distance or Time | Training Notes | Weather Conditions | Strengthening |
|---|---|---|---|---|---|
| MON | | | | T = _____ ° | |
| TUE | | | | T = _____ ° | |
| WED | | | | T = _____ ° | |
| THR | | | | T = _____ ° | |
| FRI | | | | T = _____ ° | |
| SAT | | | | T = _____ ° | |
| SUN | | | | T = _____ ° | |

Timothy E. Erson ©1993

☐ **Distance or time this week**

+ ☐ all other weeks

= ☐ New TOTAL

*Other Activities I Did This Week:*

**other** _____

S T R E T C H

# JOURNAL

*The race is not always to the swift, nor the battle to the strong.*
—Solomon

# LOG PAGE

**Training Goal:** This week I will _____

_____

HUH!

| | Date | Distance or Time | Training Notes | Weather Conditions | Strengthening |
|---|---|---|---|---|---|
| **MON** | | | | T = _____ ° | |
| **TUE** | | | | T = _____ ° | |
| **WED** | | | | T = _____ ° | |
| **THR** | | | | T = _____ ° | |
| **FRI** | | | | T = _____ ° | |
| **SAT** | | | | T = _____ ° | |
| **SUN** | | | | T = _____ ° | |

Timothy E. Erson ©1993

[ ] **Distance or time this week**

+ [ ] all other weeks

= [ ] New TOTAL

*Other Activities I Did This Week:*

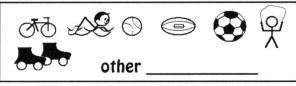

other _____

S T R E T C H

# JOURNAL

*We should not let our fears hold us back*
*from pursuing our hopes.*
—John F. Kennedy

_____

_____

_____

_____

_____

_____

_____

_____

_____

_____

_____

_____

_____

_____

_____

_____

_____

_____

# LOG PAGE

**Training Goal:** This week I will _____

_____

| | Date | Distance or Time | Training Notes | Weather Conditions | Strengthening |
|---|---|---|---|---|---|
| MON | | | | T = _____ ° | |
| TUE | | | | T = _____ ° | |
| WED | | | | T = _____ ° | |
| THR | | | | T = _____ ° | |
| FRI | | | | T = _____ ° | |
| SAT | | | | T = _____ ° | |
| SUN | | | | T = _____ ° | |

**HUH!**

Timothy E. Erson ©1993

☐ **Distance or time this week**

+ ☐ all other weeks

= ☐ New TOTAL

*Other Activities I Did This Week:*

other _____

S T R E T C H

# JOURNAL

*Keep away from people who belittle your ambition. Small people always do that, but the really great make you feel that you, too, can become great.*

—Mark Twain

# LOG PAGE

**Training Goal:** This week I will _____

_____

HUH!

| | Date | Distance or Time | Training Notes | Weather Conditions | Strengthening |
|---|---|---|---|---|---|
| **MON** | | | | T = _____ ° | |
| **TUE** | | | | T = _____ ° | |
| **WED** | | | | T = _____ ° | |
| **THR** | | | | T = _____ ° | |
| **FRI** | | | | T = _____ ° | |
| **SAT** | | | | T = _____ ° | |
| **SUN** | | | | T = _____ ° | |

Timothy E. Erson ©1993

☐ **Distance or time this week**

**+** ☐ all other weeks

**=** ☐ New TOTAL

*Other Activities I Did This Week:*

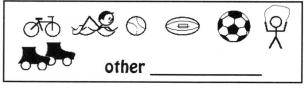

other _____

S T R E T C H

# JOURNAL

*If you can pick up after a crushing defeat, and go on to win again, you are going to be a champion someday.*

—Wilma Rudolph

# LOG PAGE

**Training Goal:** This week I will _____

_____

*HUH!*

| Date | Distance or Time | Training Notes | Weather Conditions | Strengthening |
|------|------------------|----------------|--------------------|---------------|
| **MON** | | | T = _____ ° | |
| **TUE** | | | T = _____ ° | |
| **WED** | | | T = _____ ° | |
| **THR** | | | T = _____ ° | |
| **FRI** | | | T = _____ ° | |
| **SAT** | | | T = _____ ° | |
| **SUN** | | | T = _____ ° | |

Timothy E. Erson ©1993

☐   **Distance or time this week**

\+ ☐   all other weeks

= ☐   New TOTAL

*Other Activities I Did This Week:*

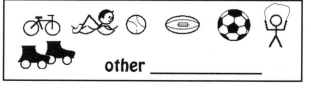

other _____

S T R E T C H

# JOURNAL

*With a little reason and much heart, one can change many things, or move mountains.*
—Albert Schweitzer

_____

_____

_____

_____

_____

_____

_____

_____

_____

_____

_____

_____

_____

_____

_____

_____

_____

_____

_____

_____

**LOG PAGE**

**Training Goal:** This week I will _____

_____

HUH!

| | Date | Distance or Time | Training Notes | Weather Conditions | Strengthening |
|---|---|---|---|---|---|
| **MON** | | | | T = _____ ° | |
| **TUE** | | | | T = _____ ° | |
| **WED** | | | | T = _____ ° | |
| **THR** | | | | T = _____ ° | |
| **FRI** | | | | T = _____ ° | |
| **SAT** | | | | T = _____ ° | |
| **SUN** | | | | T = _____ ° | |

Timothy E. Erson ©1993

☐ **Distance or time this week**

**+** ☐ all other weeks

**=** ☐ New TOTAL

*Other Activities I Did This Week:*

other _____

S T R E T C H

# JOURNAL

*Even if you're on the right track, you'll*
*get run over if you just sit there.*
—Will Rogers

## LOG PAGE

**Training Goal:** This week I will _____

_____

HUH!

| | Date | Distance or Time | Training Notes | Weather Conditions | Strengthening |
|---|---|---|---|---|---|
| MON | | | | T = _____ ° | |
| TUE | | | | T = _____ ° | |
| WED | | | | T = _____ ° | |
| THR | | | | T = _____ ° | |
| FRI | | | | T = _____ ° | |
| SAT | | | | T = _____ ° | |
| SUN | | | | T = _____ ° | |

Timothy E. Erson ©1993

☐ **Distance or time this week**

+ ☐ all other weeks

= ☐ New TOTAL

*Other Activities I Did This Week:*

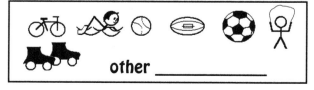

other _____

200

S—T—R—E—T—C—H

# JOURNAL

*The real challenge is not the race against others, but the race against yourself to do better.*
—Michael A. Diaz

_____

_____

_____

_____

_____

_____

_____

_____

_____

_____

_____

_____

_____

_____

_____

_____

_____

_____

_____

_____

# LOG PAGE

**Training Goal:** This week I will _____

_____

**HUH!**

| | Date | Distance or Time | Training Notes | Weather Conditions | Strengthening |
|---|---|---|---|---|---|
| **MON** | | | | T = _____ ° | |
| **TUE** | | | | T = _____ ° | |
| **WED** | | | | T = _____ ° | |
| **THR** | | | | T = _____ ° | |
| **FRI** | | | | T = _____ ° | |
| **SAT** | | | | T = _____ ° | |
| **SUN** | | | | T = _____ ° | |

Timothy E. Erson ©1993

☐ **Distance or time this week**

+ ☐ all other weeks

= ☐ New TOTAL

*Other Activities I Did This Week:*

other _____

S T R E T C H

# JOURNAL

*Nothing great was ever achieved without enthusiasm.*
—Ralph Waldo Emerson

# LOG PAGE

**Training Goal:** This week I will _____

_____

**HUH!**

| | Date | Distance or Time | Training Notes | Weather Conditions | Strengthening |
|---|---|---|---|---|---|
| MON | | | | T = _____° | |
| TUE | | | | T = _____° | |
| WED | | | | T = _____° | |
| THR | | | | T = _____° | |
| FRI | | | | T = _____° | |
| SAT | | | | T = _____° | |
| SUN | | | | T = _____° | |

Timothy E. Erson ©1993

□ **Distance or time this week**

+ □ all other weeks

= □ New TOTAL

*Other Activities I Did This Week:*

other _____

S·T·R·E·T·C·H

# JOURNAL

*It is hard to fail, but it is worse never to have tried.*
—Theodore Roosevelt

**LOG PAGE**

**Training Goal:** This week I will _____

_____

HUH!

| | Date | Distance or Time | Training Notes | Weather Conditions | Strengthening |
|---|---|---|---|---|---|
| MON | | | | T = _____ ° | |
| TUE | | | | T = _____ ° | |
| WED | | | | T = _____ ° | |
| THR | | | | T = _____ ° | |
| FRI | | | | T = _____ ° | |
| SAT | | | | T = _____ ° | |
| SUN | | | | T = _____ ° | |

Timothy E. Erson ©1993

☐ **Distance or time this week**

+ ☐ all other weeks

= ☐ New TOTAL

*Other Activities I Did This Week:*

**other** _____

S T R E T C H

# JOURNAL

*All runners are good runners—some are faster—but that's secondary. You're a winner if you participate.*
—Wade Mericle

**Training Goal:** This week I will _____

_____

| | Date | Distance or Time | Training Notes | Weather Conditions | Strengthening |
|---|---|---|---|---|---|
| MON | | | | T = _____ ° | |
| TUE | | | | T = _____ ° | |
| WED | | | | T = _____ ° | |
| THR | | | | T = _____ ° | |
| FRI | | | | T = _____ ° | |
| SAT | | | | T = _____ ° | |
| SUN | | | | T = _____ ° | |

*HUH!*

Timothy E. Erson ©1993

☐ **Distance or time this week**

+ ☐ all other weeks

= ☐ New TOTAL

*Other Activities I Did This Week:*

other _____

S T R E T C H

# JOURNAL

*If we all did things we are capable of doing,*
*we would literally astound ourselves.*
—Thomas Edison

_____

_____

_____

_____

_____

_____

_____

_____

_____

_____

_____

_____

_____

_____

_____

_____

# LOG PAGE

**Training Goal:** This week I will _____

_____

HUH!

| | Date | Distance or Time | Training Notes | Weather Conditions | Strengthening |
|---|---|---|---|---|---|
| **MON** | | | | T = _____ ° | |
| **TUE** | | | | T = _____ ° | |
| **WED** | | | | T = _____ ° | |
| **THR** | | | | T = _____ ° | |
| **FRI** | | | | T = _____ ° | |
| **SAT** | | | | T = _____ ° | |
| **SUN** | | | | T = _____ ° | |

Timothy E. Erson ©1993

☐ **Distance or time this week**

+ ☐ all other weeks

= ☐ New TOTAL

*Other Activities I Did This Week:*

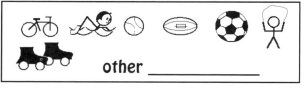

other _____

S T R E T C H

# JOURNAL

*Excellence is to do a common thing in an uncommon way.*
—Booker T. Washington

_____

_____

_____

_____

_____

_____

_____

_____

_____

_____

_____

_____

_____

_____

_____

_____

_____

_____

_____

_____

# LOG PAGE

**Training Goal:** This week I will _____

_____

HUH!

| | Date | Distance or Time | Training Notes | Weather Conditions | Strengthening |
|---|---|---|---|---|---|
| MON | | | | T = _____ ° | |
| TUE | | | | T = _____ ° | |
| WED | | | | T = _____ ° | |
| THR | | | | T = _____ ° | |
| FRI | | | | T = _____ ° | |
| SAT | | | | T = _____ ° | |
| SUN | | | | T = _____ ° | |

Timothy E. Erson ©1993

☐ **Distance or time this week**

+ ☐ all other weeks

= ☐ New TOTAL

*Other Activities I Did This Week:*

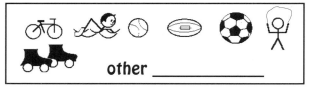

other _____

212

**S T R E T C H**

# JOURNAL

*Stick with a project to the end.  Putting it off 2 or 3 days
could end up costing you 2 or 3 weeks.*

—Leszek Sibilski

 **Training Goal:** This week I will _____

_____

HUH!

| | Date | Distance or Time | Training Notes | Weather Conditions | Strengthening |
|---|---|---|---|---|---|
| M O N | | | | T = _____ ° | |
| T U E | | | | T = _____ ° | |
| W E D | | | | T = _____ ° | |
| T H R | | | | T = _____ ° | |
| F R I | | | | T = _____ ° | |
| S A T | | | | T = _____ ° | |
| S U N | | | | T = _____ ° | |

Timothy E. Erson ©1993

☐ **Distance or time this week**

+ ☐ all other weeks

= ☐ New TOTAL

*Other Activities I Did This Week:*

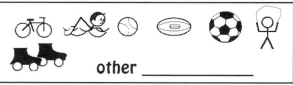

other _____

S T R E T C H

# JOURNAL

*Imagination is more important than knowledge.*
—Albert Einstein

_____

_____

_____

_____

_____

_____

_____

_____

_____

_____

_____

_____

_____

_____

_____

_____

_____

_____

_____

_____

_____

_____

**LOG PAGE**

**Training Goal:** This week I will _____
_____

HUH!

| | Date | Distance or Time | Training Notes | Weather Conditions | Strengthening |
|---|---|---|---|---|---|
| MON | | | | T = ____° | |
| TUE | | | | T = ____° | |
| WED | | | | T = ____° | |
| THR | | | | T = ____° | |
| FRI | | | | T = ____° | |
| SAT | | | | T = ____° | |
| SUN | | | | T = ____° | |

Timothy E. Erson ©1993

☐ **Distance or time this week**

+ ☐ all other weeks

= ☐ New TOTAL

*Other Activities I Did This Week:*

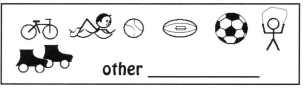

other _____

216

S-T-R-E-T-C-H

# JOURNAL

*Forgetting what lies behind, I press on*
*to what lies ahead.  I run toward the goal . . .*
—St. Paul

**LOG PAGE**

**Training Goal:** This week I will _____

_____

HUH!

| | Date | Distance or Time | Training Notes | Weather Conditions | Strengthening |
|---|---|---|---|---|---|
| **MON** | | | | T = _____ ° | |
| **TUE** | | | | T = _____ ° | |
| **WED** | | | | T = _____ ° | |
| **THR** | | | | T = _____ ° | |
| **FRI** | | | | T = _____ ° | |
| **SAT** | | | | T = _____ ° | |
| **SUN** | | | | T = _____ ° | |

Timothy E. Erson ©1993

[ ] **Distance or time this week**

+ [ ] all other weeks

= [ ] New TOTAL

*Other Activities I Did This Week:*

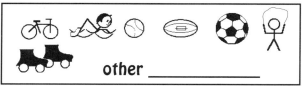

**other** _____

S T R E T C H

# JOURNAL

*It takes as much courage to have tried and failed
as it does to have tried and succeeded.*

—Anne Morrow Lindbergh

_____

_____

_____

_____

_____

_____

_____

_____

_____

_____

_____

_____

_____

_____

_____

_____

_____

_____

**LOG PAGE**

**Training Goal:** This week I will _____

_____

HUH!

| | Date | Distance or Time | Training Notes | Weather Conditions | Strengthening |
|---|---|---|---|---|---|
| **MON** | | | | T = _____ ° | |
| **TUE** | | | | T = _____ ° | |
| **WED** | | | | T = _____ ° | |
| **THR** | | | | T = _____ ° | |
| **FRI** | | | | T = _____ ° | |
| **SAT** | | | | T = _____ ° | |
| **SUN** | | | | T = _____ ° | |

Timothy E. Erson ©1993

☐ **Distance or time this week**

+ ☐ all other weeks

= ☐ New TOTAL

*Other Activities I Did This Week:*

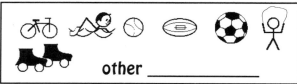

other _____

220

S T R E T C H

# JOURNAL

*I never did anything by accident nor did any of my inventions
come by accident.  They came by work.
Genius is 1% inspiration and 99% perspiration.*

—Thomas Edison

# LOG PAGE

**Training Goal:** This week I will _____

_____

HUH!

| | Date | Distance or Time | Training Notes | Weather Conditions | Strengthening |
|---|---|---|---|---|---|
| **MON** | | | | T = _____ ° | |
| **TUE** | | | | T = _____ ° | |
| **WED** | | | | T = _____ ° | |
| **THR** | | | | T = _____ ° | |
| **FRI** | | | | T = _____ ° | |
| **SAT** | | | | T = _____ ° | |
| **SUN** | | | | T = _____ ° | |

Timothy E. Erson ©1993

☐ **Distance or time this week**

+ ☐ all other weeks

= ☐ New TOTAL

*Other Activities I Did This Week:*

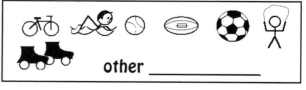

other _____

S T R E T C H

# JOURNAL

*It has been my observation that people are just about as happy as they make up their minds to be.*

—Abraham Lincoln

## LOG PAGE

**Training Goal:** This week I will _____

_____

**HUH!**

| | Date | Distance or Time | Training Notes | Weather Conditions | Strengthening |
|---|---|---|---|---|---|
| **MON** | | | | T = _____ ° | |
| **TUE** | | | | T = _____ ° | |
| **WED** | | | | T = _____ ° | |
| **THR** | | | | T = _____ ° | |
| **FRI** | | | | T = _____ ° | |
| **SAT** | | | | T = _____ ° | |
| **SUN** | | | | T = _____ ° | |

Timothy E. Erson ©1993

☐ **Distance or time this week**

+ ☐ all other weeks

= ☐ New TOTAL

*Other Activities I Did This Week:*

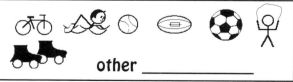

**other** _____

S T R E T C H

# JOURNAL

*Laughter is the shock absorber that takes the bumps out of life.*
—Claude Axel

**LOG PAGE**

**Training Goal:** This week I will _____

_____

| Date | Distance or Time | Training Notes | Weather Conditions | Strengthening |
|---|---|---|---|---|
| MON | | | T = _____ ° | |
| TUE | | | T = _____ ° | |
| WED | | | T = _____ ° | |
| THR | | | T = _____ ° | |
| FRI | | | T = _____ ° | |
| SAT | | | T = _____ ° | |
| SUN | | | T = _____ ° | |

HUH!

Timothy E. Erson ©1993

**Distance or time this week**

+ ☐ all other weeks

= ☐ New TOTAL

*Other Activities I Did This Week:*

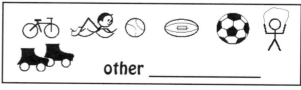

other _____

S T R E T C H

# JOURNAL

*One cannot manage too many affairs;*
*like pumpkins in the water, one pops up*
*while you try to hold down the other.*
                    —Chinese Proverb

_____

_____

_____

_____

_____

_____

_____

_____

_____

_____

_____

_____

_____

_____

_____

_____

_____

_____

_____

# LOG PAGE

**Training Goal:** This week I will _____

_____

HUH!

| | Date | Distance or Time | Training Notes | Weather Conditions | Strengthening |
|---|---|---|---|---|---|
| **MON** | | | | T = _____° | |
| **TUE** | | | | T = _____° | |
| **WED** | | | | T = _____° | |
| **THR** | | | | T = _____° | |
| **FRI** | | | | T = _____° | |
| **SAT** | | | | T = _____° | |
| **SUN** | | | | T = _____° | |

Timothy E. Erson ©1993

☐ **Distance or time this week**

+ ☐ all other weeks

= ☐ New TOTAL

*Other Activities I Did This Week:*

**other** _____

S-T-R-E-T-C-H

# JOURNAL

*Everyone has inside him a piece of good news. The good news is you don't know how great you can be! How much you can love! What you can accomplish! And what your potential is.*

—Anne Frank

_____

_____

_____

_____

_____

_____

_____

_____

_____

_____

_____

_____

_____

_____

_____

_____

_____

# LOG PAGE

**Training Goal:** This week I will _____

_____

HUH!

| | Date | Distance or Time | Training Notes | Weather Conditions | Strengthening |
|---|---|---|---|---|---|
| **MON** | | | | T = _____ ° | |
| **TUE** | | | | T = _____ ° | |
| **WED** | | | | T = _____ ° | |
| **THR** | | | | T = _____ ° | |
| **FRI** | | | | T = _____ ° | |
| **SAT** | | | | T = _____ ° | |
| **SUN** | | | | T = _____ ° | |

Timothy E. Erson ©1993

☐ **Distance or time this week**

**+** ☐ all other weeks

**=** ☐ New TOTAL

*Other Activities I Did This Week:*

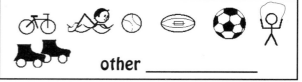

other _____

230

S T R E T C H

# JOURNAL

*Last Sunday more than 8,000 of us started on a mighty walk
from Selma, Alabama. . . . Our bodies are tired, our feet
are somewhat sore . . . our souls are rested.*

—Martin Luther King, Jr.

**LOG PAGE**

**Training Goal:** This week I will _____

_____

HUH!

| | Date | Distance or Time | Training Notes | Weather Conditions | Strengthening |
|---|---|---|---|---|---|
| MON | | | | T = _____ ° | |
| TUE | | | | T = _____ ° | |
| WED | | | | T = _____ ° | |
| THR | | | | T = _____ ° | |
| FRI | | | | T = _____ ° | |
| SAT | | | | T = _____ ° | |
| SUN | | | | T = _____ ° | |

☐ **Distance or time this week**

+ ☐ all other weeks

= ☐ New TOTAL

*Other Activities I Did This Week:*

other _____

S-T-R-E-T-C-H

Timothy E. Erson ©1993

# JOURNAL

*A faithful friend is a sure shelter.  Whoever has found one has found a rare treasure.*

—Solomon

## LOG PAGE

**Training Goal:** This week I will _____

_____

**HUH!**

| | Date | Distance or Time | Training Notes | Weather Conditions | Strengthening |
|---|---|---|---|---|---|
| **MON** | | | | T = _____ ° | |
| **TUE** | | | | T = _____ ° | |
| **WED** | | | | T = _____ ° | |
| **THR** | | | | T = _____ ° | |
| **FRI** | | | | T = _____ ° | |
| **SAT** | | | | T = _____ ° | |
| **SUN** | | | | T = _____ ° | |

Timothy E. Erson ©1993

☐ **Distance or time this week**

+ ☐ all other weeks

= ☐ New TOTAL

*Other Activities I Did This Week:*

**other** _____

234

**S T R E T C H**

# JOURNAL

*I find in running—win or lose—a deep satisfaction
that I cannot express in any other way.*
—Roger Bannister

_____

_____

_____

_____

_____

_____

_____

_____

_____

_____

_____

_____

_____

_____

_____

_____

_____

_____

_____

_____

# LOG PAGE

**Training Goal:** This week I will _____

_____

_HUH!_

| | Date | Distance or Time | Training Notes | Weather Conditions | Strengthening |
|---|---|---|---|---|---|
| MON | | | | T = _____° | |
| TUE | | | | T = _____° | |
| WED | | | | T = _____° | |
| THR | | | | T = _____° | |
| FRI | | | | T = _____° | |
| SAT | | | | T = _____° | |
| SUN | | | | T = _____° | |

Timothy E. Erson ©1993

☐ **Distance or time this week**

+ ☐ all other weeks

= ☐ New TOTAL

_Other Activities I Did This Week:_

other _____

236

**S T R E T C H**

# JOURNAL

*Life is an exciting business, and most exciting
when it is lived for others.*
—Helen Keller

# LOG PAGE

**Training Goal:** This week I will _____

_____

HUH!

| | Date | Distance or Time | Training Notes | Weather Conditions | Strengthening |
|---|---|---|---|---|---|
| MON | | | | T = _____° | |
| TUE | | | | T = _____° | |
| WED | | | | T = _____° | |
| THR | | | | T = _____° | |
| FRI | | | | T = _____° | |
| SAT | | | | T = _____° | |
| SUN | | | | T = _____° | |

☐ **Distance or time this week**

**+** ☐ all other weeks

**=** ☐ New TOTAL

*Other Activities I Did This Week:*

other _____

238

S T R E T C H

# JOURNAL

*Our greatest glory is not in never falling,*
*but in rising every time we fall.*
—Confucius

_____

_____

_____

_____

_____

_____

_____

_____

_____

_____

_____

_____

_____

_____

_____

_____

_____

_____

**Training Goal:** This week I will _____

_____

| | Date | Distance or Time | Training Notes | Weather Conditions | Strengthening HUH! |
|---|---|---|---|---|---|
| **M O N** | | | | ☀ T = ___ ° | |
| **T U E** | | | | ☀ T = ___ ° | |
| **W E D** | | | | ☀ T = ___ ° | |
| **T H R** | | | | ☀ T = ___ ° | |
| **F R I** | | | | ☀ T = ___ ° | |
| **S A T** | | | | ☀ T = ___ ° | |
| **S U N** | | | | ☀ T = ___ ° | |

Timothy E. Erson ©1993

[ ] **Distance or time this week**

+ [ ] all other weeks

= [ ] New TOTAL

*Other Activities I Did This Week:*

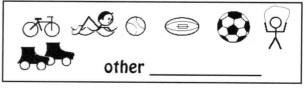

other _____

240

S T R E T C H

# JOURNAL

*If we walk long enough and if we talk long enough,
we might get to understand one another.*
—Jesse Owens

# LOG PAGE

**Training Goal:** This week I will _____

_____

HUH!

| | Date | Distance or Time | Training Notes | Weather Conditions | Strengthening |
|---|---|---|---|---|---|
| MON | | | | T = _____ ° | |
| TUE | | | | T = _____ ° | |
| WED | | | | T = _____ ° | |
| THR | | | | T = _____ ° | |
| FRI | | | | T = _____ ° | |
| SAT | | | | T = _____ ° | |
| SUN | | | | T = _____ ° | |

Timothy E. Erson ©1993

☐ **Distance or time this week**

+ ☐ all other weeks

= ☐ New TOTAL

*Other Activities I Did This Week:*

other _____

S  T  R  E  T  C  H

# JOURNAL

*Little by little does the trick.*

—Aesop

_____

_____

_____

_____

_____

_____

_____

_____

_____

_____

_____

_____

_____

_____

_____

_____

_____

_____

_____

# LOG PAGE

**Training Goal:** This week I will _____

_____

**HUH!**

| | Date | Distance or Time | Training Notes | Weather Conditions | Strengthening |
|---|---|---|---|---|---|
| MON | | | | T = _____ ° | |
| TUE | | | | T = _____ ° | |
| WED | | | | T = _____ ° | |
| THR | | | | T = _____ ° | |
| FRI | | | | T = _____ ° | |
| SAT | | | | T = _____ ° | |
| SUN | | | | T = _____ ° | |

Timothy E. Erson ©1993

☐ **Distance or time this week**

+ ☐ all other weeks

= ☐ New TOTAL

*Other Activities I Did This Week:*

**other** _____

S T R E T C H

# JOURNAL

*You win only if you aren't afraid to lose.*
—Rocky Aoki

_____

_____

_____

_____

_____

_____

_____

_____

_____

_____

_____

_____

_____

_____

_____

_____

_____

_____

**LOG PAGE**

**Training Goal:** This week I will _____

_____

| | Date | Distance or Time | Training Notes | Weather Conditions | Strengthening **HUH!** |
|---|---|---|---|---|---|
| **MON** | | | | T = _____ ° | |
| **TUE** | | | | T = _____ ° | |
| **WED** | | | | T = _____ ° | |
| **THR** | | | | T = _____ ° | |
| **FRI** | | | | T = _____ ° | |
| **SAT** | | | | T = _____ ° | |
| **SUN** | | | | T = _____ ° | |

Timothy E. Erson ©1993

☐ **Distance or time this week**

+ ☐ all other weeks

= ☐ New TOTAL

*Other Activities I Did This Week:*

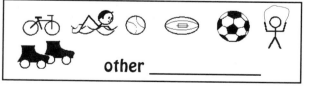

other _____

246

**S T R E T C H**

# JOURNAL

*We know what we are, but know not what we may be.*
—William Shakespeare

_____

_____

_____

_____

_____

_____

_____

_____

_____

_____

_____

_____

_____

_____

_____

_____

_____

_____

## LOG PAGE

**Training Goal:** This week I will _____

_____

**HUH!**

| | Date | Distance or Time | Training Notes | Weather Conditions | Strengthening |
|---|---|---|---|---|---|
| **MON** | | | | T = _____ ° | |
| **TUE** | | | | T = _____ ° | |
| **WED** | | | | T = _____ ° | |
| **THR** | | | | T = _____ ° | |
| **FRI** | | | | T = _____ ° | |
| **SAT** | | | | T = _____ ° | |
| **SUN** | | | | T = _____ ° | |

[ ] **Distance or time this week**

+ [ ] all other weeks

= [ ] New TOTAL

*Other Activities I Did This Week:*

other _____

Timothy E. Erson ©1993

S T R E T C H

# JOURNAL

*The day you take complete responsibility for yourself, the day you stop making any excuses, that's the day you start to the top.*

—O. J. Simpson

**LOG PAGE**

**Training Goal:** This week I will _____

_____

HUH!

| | Date | Distance or Time | Training Notes | Weather Conditions | Strengthening |
|---|---|---|---|---|---|
| M O N | | | | T = _____ ° | |
| T U E | | | | T = _____ ° | |
| W E D | | | | T = _____ ° | |
| T H R | | | | T = _____ ° | |
| F R I | | | | T = _____ ° | |
| S A T | | | | T = _____ ° | |
| S U N | | | | T = _____ ° | |

Timothy E. Erson ©1993

[ ] **Distance or time this week**

+ [ ] all other weeks

= [ ] New TOTAL

*Other Activities I Did This Week:*

**other** _____

250

S T R E T C H

# JOURNAL

*Friendship is the only cement*
*that will ever hold the world together.*
—Woodrow Wilson

**LOG PAGE**

**Training Goal:** This week I will _____

_____

**HUH!**

| | Date | Distance or Time | Training Notes | Weather Conditions | Strengthening |
|---|---|---|---|---|---|
| **MON** | | | | T = _____ ° | |
| **TUE** | | | | T = _____ ° | |
| **WED** | | | | T = _____ ° | |
| **THR** | | | | T = _____ ° | |
| **FRI** | | | | T = _____ ° | |
| **SAT** | | | | T = _____ ° | |
| **SUN** | | | | T = _____ ° | |

[ ] **Distance or time this week**

+ [ ] all other weeks

= [ ] New TOTAL

*Other Activities I Did This Week:*

other _____

**252**

**S T R E T C H**

# JOURNAL

*The most important thing in life is not the triumph
but the struggle.  The essential thing is not to have
conquered but to have fought well.*

—Baron Pierre de Coubertin
(part of the Olympic creed)

_____

_____

_____

_____

_____

_____

_____

_____

_____

_____

_____

_____

_____

_____

_____

_____

_____

_____

# LOG PAGE

**Training Goal:** This week I will _____

_____

*HUH!*

| | Date | Distance or Time | Training Notes | Weather Conditions | Strengthening |
|---|---|---|---|---|---|
| MON | | | | T = _____ ° | |
| TUE | | | | T = _____ ° | |
| WED | | | | T = _____ ° | |
| THR | | | | T = _____ ° | |
| FRI | | | | T = _____ ° | |
| SAT | | | | T = _____ ° | |
| SUN | | | | T = _____ ° | |

Timothy E. Erson ©1993

☐ **Distance or time this week**

+ ☐ all other weeks

= ☐ New TOTAL

*Other Activities I Did This Week:*

**other** _____

254

S-T-R-E-T-C-H

# JOURNAL

*Never never never never give up.*
—Winston Churchill

# RACE LOG

| Date | Event/Distance | Time | Weather Conditions |
|------|----------------|------|--------------------|
|      |                |      | Temperature _____ |

**Comments** _____

_____

_____

| Date | Event/Distance | Time | Weather Conditions |
|------|----------------|------|--------------------|
|      |                |      | Temperature _____ |

**Comments** _____

_____

_____

257

| Date | Event/Distance | Time | Weather Conditions |
|------|----------------|------|--------------------|
|      |                |      | Temperature _____ ° |

**Comments** _____

_____

_____

| Date | Event/Distance | Time | Weather Conditions |
|------|----------------|------|--------------------|
|      |                |      | Temperature _____ ° |

**Comments** _____

_____

_____

| Date | Event/Distance | Time | Weather Conditions |
|------|----------------|------|--------------------|
|      |                |      | Temperature _____ ° |

**Comments** _____

_____

_____

| Date | Event/Distance | Time | Weather Conditions |
|------|----------------|------|--------------------|
|      |                |      | Temperature _____ ° |

**Comments** _____

_____

_____

| Date | Event/Distance | Time | Weather Conditions |
|------|----------------|------|--------------------|
|      |                |      | Temperature _____ ° |

**Comments** _____

_____

_____

| Date | Event/Distance | Time | Weather Conditions |
|------|----------------|------|--------------------|
|      |                |      | Temperature _____ ° |

**Comments** _____

_____

_____

| Date | Event/Distance | Time | Weather Conditions |
|------|----------------|------|--------------------|
|      |                |      | |
|      |                |      | Temperature _____ |
| **Comments** _____ |
| _____ |
| _____ |

| Date | Event/Distance | Time | Weather Conditions |
|------|----------------|------|--------------------|
|      |                |      | |
|      |                |      | Temperature _____ |
| **Comments** _____ |
| _____ |
| _____ |

| Date | Event/Distance | Time | Weather Conditions |
|------|----------------|------|--------------------|
|      |                |      | |
|      |                |      | Temperature _____ |
| **Comments** _____ |
| _____ |
| _____ |

| Date | Event/Distance | Time | Weather Conditions |
|------|----------------|------|--------------------|
|  |  |  | |
| **Comments** _____ | | | |
| _____ | | | |
| _____ | | | |

Temperature _____

| Date | Event/Distance | Time | Weather Conditions |
|------|----------------|------|--------------------|
|  |  |  | |
| **Comments** _____ | | | |
| _____ | | | |
| _____ | | | |

Temperature _____

| Date | Event/Distance | Time | Weather Conditions |
|------|----------------|------|--------------------|
|  |  |  | |
| **Comments** _____ | | | |
| _____ | | | |
| _____ | | | |

Temperature _____

| Date | Event/Distance | Time | Weather Conditions |
|------|----------------|------|--------------------|
|      |                |      | Temperature _____ |

**Comments** _____

_____

_____

| Date | Event/Distance | Time | Weather Conditions |
|------|----------------|------|--------------------|
|      |                |      | Temperature _____ |

**Comments** _____

_____

_____

| Date | Event/Distance | Time | Weather Conditions |
|------|----------------|------|--------------------|
|      |                |      | Temperature _____ |

**Comments** _____

_____

_____

| Date | Event/Distance | Time | Weather Conditions |
|------|----------------|------|--------------------|
|      |                |      | Temperature _____ |

**Comments** _____

_____

_____

| Date | Event/Distance | Time | Weather Conditions |
|------|----------------|------|--------------------|
|      |                |      | Temperature _____ |

**Comments** _____

_____

_____

| Date | Event/Distance | Time | Weather Conditions |
|------|----------------|------|--------------------|
|      |                |      | Temperature _____ |

**Comments** _____

_____

_____

Answers to **Math Miles:**

1. 16    2. 8    3.a. 360    3.b. 14.7    Bonus: 51.5